ISRAEL RISING

DOUG HERSHEY

Photography Elise Theriault

CITADEL PRESS
Kensington Publishing Corp.
www.kensingtonbooks.com

DEDICATION:

To my amazing children, Elijah, Josiah, Levi, and Rachel. Each of you is a unique treasure to me and you are loved more than you know! May you live to see the completed fulfillment of these promises with your own eyes; may it stir your heart to be a part of this miraculous restoration, and may it change you forever. ~ Abba

CITADEL PRESS BOOKS are published by

Kensington Publishing Corp.
119 West 40th Street
New York, NY 10018

Copyright © 2018 Doug Hershey

Design and production by Koechel Peterson and Associates, Minneapolis, Minnesota

All rights reserved. No part of this book may be reproduced in any form or by any means without the prior written consent of the publisher, excepting brief quotes used in reviews.

All Scripture quotations, unless otherwise indicated, are taken from the Holy Bible, New International Version®, NIV®. Copyright ©1973, 1978, 1984, 2011 by Biblica, Inc.™ Used by permission of Zondervan. All rights reserved worldwide. www.zondervan.com The "NIV" and "New International Version" are trademarks registered in the United States Patent and Trademark Office by Biblica, Inc.™

All Kensington titles, imprints, and distributed lines are available at special quantity discounts for bulk purchases for sales promotions, premiums, fund-raising, educational, or institutional use.

Special book excerpts or customized printings can also be created to fit specific needs. For details, write or phone the office of the Kensington sales manager: Kensington Publishing Corp., 119 West 40th Street, New York, New York 10018, attn.: Sales Department; phone 1-800-221-2647.

The publisher does not assume any responsibility for the opinions or views of the author, nor for third-party websites or their content or accessibility.

CITADEL PRESS and the Citadel logo are Reg. U.S. Pat. & TM Off.

ISBN-13: 978-0-8065-3907-2
ISBN-10: 0-8065-3907-0

First Citadel hardcover printing: April 2018

10 9 8 7 6 5 4 3 2 1

Printed in the United States of America

Library of Congress CIP data is available.

First electronic edition: April 2018

CONTENTS

Introduction	6
The Ancient Prophecy	
Ezekiel Chapter 36	8
The History of the Land	12
Camera Obscura	15
Mark Twain	18
The Modern Lens	
Galilee and Golan	23
Jezreel Valley	52
Judea and Samaria	68
Coastal Plain	102
The Negev Desert	141
Center	169
Jerusalem	176
Conclusion	200
Reference: Historical Eye Witness Accounts of the Land from the 4–19th Centuries	202

SPECIAL THANKS

All of my crowd funding backers, great and small, my grateful thanks for your excitement, support, and patience after funding this project. Mary and Lee Wolff, Ian Jupp and Jimmy Nimon—your belief in this project idea and initial gifts of "matching funds" for our fundraising campaign made it a huge success. Elise, from the beginning, your hard work, creative eye, and unique perspective captured some of the most stunning photos I've ever seen of Israel. It's great work! Todd Bolen/Bibleplaces.com for permission to use the American Colony black-and-white photo collections. The Eilat Museum/Shmulik Taggar for sharing some of your old Eilat collections, Dan Alon, Gili Yahav and Mayor of Mitzpe Ramon, Roni Marom for sharing the old photos of beginnings of the town. Yochanan Marcellino/City of Peace Media, without your experience and understanding of the book's prophetic vision for Israel's 70th anniversary, I would not have gotten so far so fast.

John Peterson & David Koechel of KPA (Koechel Peterson & Associates) for your incredible design work and for running with the vision of *Israel Rising* with Godspeed, Gregory Rohm and Sara Marino at KPA for all their hard work and dedication, Steve Zacharius & Lynn Cully of Kensington Publishing/Citadel Press for your wisdom, leadership, and unwavering belief in the *Israel Rising* project. Denise Silvestro, for your hard work, wisdom, and insight in directing this book at Citadel Press. Sam Noerr, Noerr Creative, for all your creative help in moving *Israel Rising* to the finish line. Sam Interrante, for the awesome headshots. Jordan Marcellino, The Beautiful Land Initiative (BLI), for sharing your sacrificial heart of active participation in the land's awakening. Chaim Malespin/Aliyah Return Center, for our red sign adventures, our conversations of fulfilling prophecies, and providing a place for the restoration of the Jewish people in the land. Rabbi Naphtali ("Tuly") Weisz of Israel365.com for your friendship, overwhelming support, and for being a living example and fulfillment of Ezekiel 36.

Most importantly, to the Lord, Who am I that I live in a day to see Your ancient faithful promises coming to pass in the earth just as You said. Thank you for dropping this vision in my heart, providing the path forward, and allowing me to complete it. May I continue to see your faithfulness to your promises and say, *"For He is good, for His lovingkindness is upon Israel forever"* (Ezra 3:11).

FOREWORD

One of the greatest aspects of living in the State of Israel is the blessing to witness the Bible come to life before your very eyes. Each day my wife and I can't believe we are fortunate to be the first generation of our families to raise our children in the Land of Israel since our people were exiled thousands of years ago.

Having moved to Israel from America a few years ago, we live in a neighborhood of Jewish immigrants from the four corners of the world as described by Isaiah 49. We marvel when our kids play in the streets in fulfillment of Zechariah 8, and we laugh when we hear Hebrew spoken in the shops as foretold by Zephaniah 3. From the beginning until the end of the year, we are so fortunate to participate in these great miracles.

After making Aliyah, I started Israel365 inspired by Deuteronomy 11:12: "It is a land the LORD your God cares for; the eyes of the LORD your God are continually on it from the beginning of the year to its end." Here the Bible describes what God does each and every day: He looks upon the Land of Israel! Israel365 became my way to share with others all over the world the physical beauty and the biblical significance of Israel, 365 days a year. I am therefore so grateful to Doug Hershey for presenting *Israel Rising: Ancient Prophecy/ Modern Lens*.

Doug Hershey's phenomenal new book, *Israel Rising: Ancient Prophecy/Modern Lens: The Land of Israel Reawakens"* presents a dramatic and vivid portrayal of God's incredible blessings upon Israel over the past century. On page after beautiful page, "Ancient prophecy/Modern Lens" bears testimony to God's eternal covenant with the Land and the People of Israel.

While *Israel Rising* contains many inspiring passages from the Torah, when I see the sharp contrast between the old and new images Doug Hershey presents, I am reminded of the words of the prophet Isaiah: "Shake off your dust; rise up, sit enthroned, Jerusalem" (Isaiah 52:2). The prophet describes a future day when the former glory of Jerusalem will be revealed. The ancient beauty of the holy city and the Promised Land that were concealed for centuries will shake off their dust and rise again.

Each of us has a part to play in the unfolding of prophecy and the restoration of Israel. I am glad Doug Hershey used his immense creativity to combine Elise's photographs and his literary skills to capture the glorious redemption of Israel. We can all benefit from *Israel Rising* to greater appreciate what God is doing for Israel in our generation, in front of our very eyes.

With blessings from Israel,
RABBI TULY WEISZ, Israel365

INTRODUCTION

One of my favorite drives in Israel is by way of Hwy 90 that follows the Jordan River between the Sea of Galilee and the Dead Sea. The first time I drove this road in the late 1990s, I was struck by the transformation in the landscape while driving south. Upon leaving the plush and fertile farmland of Galilee, the brown hues of the desert soon began growing more expansive and rocks began changing. Somehow the sun seemed more intense, and in a short amount of time, it became quite evident that I was in a different world. Back then, aside from a few tiny villages and small subsistence farms in the desert, the barren landscape of browns, tans, and beige colors wrestled with one another for what felt like hours. Then suddenly it all changed when I crested a hill near ancient Jericho and I was welcomed by a sea of green and a true oasis in the desert.

Today this same stretch of highway is very different and is now part of a growing miracle. The desert is shrinking due to the explosion of desert farming techniques, revolutionary irrigation systems, and—for the first time in many centuries—a growing population. This same desert drive that used to be brown and dusty is now being overtaken by the life-giving colors of orchards, vineyards, greenhouses, small fields, and thriving communities. It has been an eye-opening opportunity to see this change happen firsthand. While it's great to read about such dramatic changes, it's something you simply need to see—thus the reason for this book. Perhaps more intriguing is that this change was prophesied over 2600 years ago.

In the late sixth century BC, the biblical prophet Ezekiel spoke a message directly to the physical land of his forefathers. He foretold a day when the desolate barren homeland of his ancestors would put forth branches and produce fruit, that the land would be cultivated and sown with all kinds of crops, that the ruined and forsaken cities would again be rebuilt and inhabited, that man and beast would be multiplied on it, and that the land would come alive as never before. Ezekiel even gave signposts of when and how these miraculous transformations would happen. Since the time that Ezekiel spoke these words, this land has been conquered and reconquered multitudes of times by several world empires. Uncountable numbers of men were slain upon it. The landscape was plundered and made desolate, stripped of its fertility and value. That is until recent generations when some unique changes began to take place.

To help facilitate this dramatic view of history, we will start at the beginning. We will look at what exactly Ezekiel prophesied, including his time frame and the parameters that he set down for the fulfillment of his remarkable words. We will read the historical accounts from Jewish, Christian, and Muslim eyewitnesses who detail what the land and region looked like and has experienced and endured, spanning several empires in the last 2000 years. Thanks to the invention of the modern camera and pioneering photographers in the late 1800s, we will view the land that they walked and photographed from the 1880s–1940s, and then compare them to new, present-day photos of the same locations that include insightful facts.

The majority of the old photos in this book are from the "American Colony: Eric Matson Collection," as it is one of the best and well-preserved photo collections of the region. We started with over 2200 old photos taken between the 1880s and the 1940s at locations all over Israel, in what was then the Ottoman Empire and later British Mandate Palestine. Those photos were then culled to a couple hundred of the best city and landscape photo shots to be recreated to the best of our ability. Our team attempted to photograph using the exact same angle that the photographers had captured generations before us. Whenever possible, we tried to line up the landscape lines so that they were identical to the original photograph, so as to help orient the viewer to the changes that have taken place since then in the area. At times, due to the growth of cities and vegetation, we simply could not use the exact angle, so the next best possible angle was selected. While there are lots of stunning things to photograph in Israel, we used the old photos from the collection as our primary roadmap. In time, these little treasure hunts to find the exact spot of the original photo became one of the most exciting aspects of this project, since it required the help of curious and willing locals, both Jewish and Arab.

The human aspect quickly became a welcomed, yet unexpected, element of this project. Landscapes simply don't change on their own, but rather through the efforts of the people caring for it. These encounters, detours and, at times, seemingly "divine appointments" were so compelling that I included some short blog style entries as part of our journey on our way to recreating these historic photographs. As you will see, the people are a prime component of Ezekiel's prophecy. Whether knowingly or unknowingly, it's through their hands that these changes have come about. In the pages ahead, you will see cities that sprang out of nowhere, forgotten ruins now inhabited centuries later, barren mountains now covered with verdant trees, and desolate plains now transformed into fertile farmlands. All made possible by the people who had a heart for the land of their forefathers and felt drawn back to it.

There will be photos of places you may recognize and places you've never even heard of. This is intentional. While entire photo books could be created of a particular city such as Jerusalem, which has a rich history and extensive photo archives, we chose to cover the land as a whole. For this reason, much of a location's deep history will not be covered, and many popular old photo angles will not be used. We want to show our readers locations and angles that few have ever seen. Throughout the land, the transformations are truly stunning; something that needs to be seen to be believed.

In today's world of Middle Eastern politics involving land disputes and religious tensions, my aim is not a political statement or a religious declaration. Rather, let's consider the facts that suggest that something miraculously tangible is currently unfolding in our day that was foretold over two millennia ago and view the photos that seem to prove it. While there are many "then/now" photo books that could be published about any city or country in the world, none of those places' revival was foretold by an ancient prophet with such exact detail. That fact alone should compel us to look deeper.

Let's take an honest look at this ancient prophecy, consider the 2000 years of eyewitness accounts that verify what the old photos depict, compare them using our modern photo lens of today, then come to our own conclusions. By the end, my hope is that the reader would ask perhaps the most important question: "How and why is this happening?"

Welcome to the unfolding journey of *Israel Rising: Ancient Prophecy/Modern Lens*.

~Doug Hershey

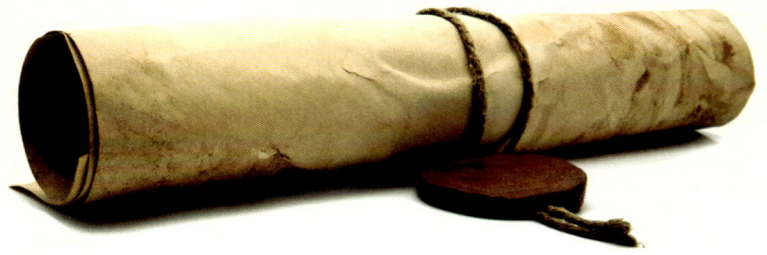

THE ANCIENT PROPHECY:
Ezekiel Chapter 36

My journey began with this ancient passage. While I had read it before, it really didn't attract my attention until I began recognizing portions of the Jordan Valley changing firsthand, within a short fifteen-year time period. I began to wonder, "Could this really be connected to what Ezekiel was talking about?" I had to go back and take a closer look.

The prophet Ezekiel was part of the Jewish population of Jerusalem that was taken captive and relocated during the Babylonian conquest in 597 BC as described in the Bible. After several years of living in Babylon, he began receiving prophetic messages from God and addressed them to the Jewish exiles. Here is a portion of one of those prophecies.

"Son of man, prophesy to the mountains of Israel and say, 'Mountains of Israel, hear the word of the Lord. [2] This is what the Sovereign Lord says: The enemy said of you, "Aha! The ancient heights have become our possession."'[3] Therefore prophesy and say, 'This is what the Sovereign Lord says: Because they ravaged and crushed you from every side so that you became the possession of the rest of the nations and the object of people's malicious talk and slander,[4] therefore, mountains of Israel, hear the word of the Sovereign Lord: This is what the Sovereign Lord says to the mountains and hills, to the ravines and valleys, to the desolate ruins and the deserted towns that have been plundered and ridiculed by the rest of the nations around you—[5] this is what the Sovereign Lord says: In my burning zeal I have spoken against the rest of the nations, and against all Edom, for with glee and with malice in their hearts they made my land their own possession so that they might plunder its pastureland.'[6] Therefore prophesy concerning the land of Israel and say to the mountains and hills, to the ravines and valleys: 'This is what the Sovereign Lord says: I speak in my jealous wrath because you have suffered the scorn of the nations.[7] Therefore this is what the Sovereign Lord says: I swear with uplifted hand that the nations around you will also suffer scorn.

[8] *"'But you, mountains of Israel, will produce branches and fruit for my people Israel, for they will soon come home.[9] I am concerned for you and will look*

on you with favor; you will be plowed and sown, ¹⁰ *and I will cause many people to live on you—yes, all of Israel. The towns will be inhabited and the ruins rebuilt.* ¹¹ *I will increase the number of people and animals living on you, and they will be fruitful and become numerous. I will settle people on you as in the past and will make you prosper more than before. Then you will know that I am the LORD.* ¹² *I will cause people, my people Israel, to live on you. They will possess you, and you will be their inheritance; you will never again deprive them of their children.*

¹³ *"'This is what the Sovereign LORD says: Because some say to you, "You devour people and deprive your nation of its children,"* ¹⁴ *therefore you will no longer devour people or make your nation childless, declares the Sovereign LORD.* ¹⁵ *No longer will I make you hear the taunts of the nations, and no longer will you suffer the scorn of the peoples or cause your nation to fall, declares the Sovereign LORD.'"*

¹⁶ *Again the word of the LORD came to me:* ¹⁷ *"Son of man, when the people of Israel were living in their own land, they defiled it by their conduct and their actions. Their conduct was like a woman's monthly uncleanness in my sight.* ¹⁸ *So I poured out my wrath on them because they had shed blood in the land and because they had defiled it with their idols.* ¹⁹ *I dispersed them among the nations, and they were scattered through the countries; I judged them according to their conduct and their actions.* ²⁰ *And wherever they went among the nations they profaned my holy name, for it was said of them, 'These are the LORD's people, and yet they had to leave his land.'* ²¹ *I had concern for my holy name, which the people of Israel profaned among the nations where they had gone.*

²² *"Therefore say to the Israelites, 'This is what the Sovereign LORD says: It is not for your sake, people of Israel, that I am going to do these things, but for the sake of my holy name, which you have profaned among the nations where you have gone.* ²³ *I will show the holiness of my great name, which has been profaned among the nations, the name you have profaned among them. Then the nations will know that I am the LORD, declares the Sovereign LORD, when I am proved holy through you before their eyes.*

²⁴ *"'For I will take you out of the nations; I will gather you from all the countries and bring you back into your own land.* ²⁵ *I will sprinkle clean water on you, and you will be clean; I will cleanse you from all your impurities and from all your idols.* ²⁶ *I will give you a new heart and put a new spirit in you; I will remove from you your heart of stone and give you a heart of flesh.* ²⁷ *And I will put my Spirit in you and move you to follow my decrees and be careful to keep my laws.* ²⁸ *Then you will live in the land I gave your ancestors; you will be my people, and I will be your God.* ²⁹ *I will save you from all your uncleanness. I will call for the grain and make it plentiful and will not bring famine upon you.* ³⁰ *I will increase the fruit of the trees and the crops of the field, so that you will no longer suffer disgrace among the nations because of famine.* ³¹ *Then you will remember your evil ways and wicked deeds, and you will loathe yourselves for your sins and detestable practices.* ³² *I want you to know that I am not doing this for your sake, declares the Sovereign LORD. Be ashamed and disgraced for your conduct, people of Israel!*

³³ *"'This is what the Sovereign LORD says: On the day I cleanse you from all your sins, I will resettle your towns, and the ruins will be rebuilt.* ³⁴ *The desolate land will be cultivated instead of lying desolate in the sight of all who pass through it.* ³⁵ *They will say, "This land that was laid waste has become like the garden of Eden; the cities that were lying in ruins, desolate and destroyed, are now fortified and inhabited."* ³⁶ *Then the nations around you that remain will know that I the LORD have rebuilt what was destroyed and have replanted what was desolate. I the LORD have spoken, and I will do it.'*

³⁷ *"This is what the Sovereign LORD says: Once again I will yield to Israel's plea and do this for them: I will make their people as numerous as sheep,* ³⁸ *as numerous as the flocks for offerings at Jerusalem during her appointed festivals. So will the ruined cities be filled with flocks of people. Then they will know that I am the LORD."*

While there is much that could be said about this portion of Scripture on a variety of topics, for my own understanding, I simplified its key details into four easy questions: (1) Who is this spoken to?; (2) Why was it spoken?; (3) What will happen?; and (4) When will it all come to pass?

WHO IS THIS PROPHECY SPOKEN TO?

We tend to think of prophecies being spoken to nations, kings, or—quite simply—people. What makes this prophecy unique is that Ezekiel is instructed to prophesy to the physical land of Israel and speak to it as an actual living being. This can be seen in the first several verses, starting with the very first sentence:

"Son of man, prophesy to the mountains of Israel and say, 'Mountains of Israel, hear the word of the LORD." (v. 1)

"…therefore, mountains of Israel, hear the word of the Sovereign LORD: This is what the Sovereign LORD says to the mountains and hills, to the ravines and valleys, to the desolate ruins and the deserted towns that have been plundered and ridiculed by the rest of the nations around you…" (v. 4)

"Therefore prophesy concerning the land of Israel and say to the mountains and hills, to the ravines and valleys…" (v. 6)

"Listen up, you mountains, hills, ravines, valleys, and desolate places of Israel—this word is spoken to you." We, as human beings reading these words, are simply bystanders to the message Ezekiel gave prophetically. As we read this passage, keep in mind that when we read the word "you" in the first fifteen verses, it's talking to the physical land of Israel, not Israel as a people or nation. But why was this spoken to the land and not the people?

WHY WAS THIS PROPHECY SPOKEN TO THE LAND?

This question is best answered in two parts. Yet, both parts of the answer suggest that there seems to be something unique about the land and how it is treated. Throughout this passage, we find three different references about the ownership of the land:

*"…they made **my land** their own possession…"* (v. 5)

*"…it was said of them, 'These are the LORD's people, and yet they had to leave **his land**.'"* (v. 20)

*"Then you will live in **the land I gave** your ancestors; you will be my people, and I will be your God."* (v. 28)

As God is speaking to Ezekiel, the land is called *"My land, His land, and the land He gave."* This is not just any piece of real estate. It appears to be something that is extremely significant to God Himself. This being the case, it stands to reason that He cares about the land's treatment, condition, and its ownership.

It is widely believed and accepted that Jews are "God's chosen people." Where that idea originated from is God's encounter with Abraham found in Genesis 17, when God made an everlasting covenant with Abraham. Yet in that same everlasting promise, there is a second element that is often overlooked.

"[7] I will establish my covenant as an everlasting covenant between me and you and your descendants after you for the generations to come, to be your God and the God of your descendants after you. [8] The whole land of Canaan, where you now reside as a foreigner, I will give as an everlasting possession to you and your descendants after you; and I will be their God." (Genesis 17:7–8)

In the same conversation stating that Abraham's descendants would be part of an everlasting covenant (repeated later to Abraham's sons Isaac and Jacob), the promise of the land as an everlasting possession immediately follows. Quite simply, the land is part of the everlasting covenant that is inseparable from the people. Perhaps this is why there was such distain in this prophecy for how other nations had treated the land.

According to Ezekiel 36, the reason for this prophecy was because the land had not been treated well and had been stolen by invading nations.

"This is what the Sovereign LORD says: The enemy said of you, "Aha! The ancient heights have become our possession." (v. 2)

"…they ravaged and crushed you from every side so that you became the possession of the rest of the nations" (v. 3)

"'...for with glee and with malice in their hearts they made my land their own possession so that they might plunder its pastureland.'" (v. 5)

The invading nations took possession of and laid waste to the land. These were wrongs that needed correcting, thus the purpose of the message. But what exactly would change and happen?

WHAT CHANGES WILL HAPPEN TO THE LAND?

In its most basic elements, any land is intended to sustain a population, bring forth food, and provide materials for shelter. It is intended to be a help to those who live on it. Around the world, "good land" is soil that can be worked to feed and sustain a local population with its benefits, while arid deserts have few natural resources that can sustain life. God was speaking to a land that was made desolate, was crushed, and openly plundered. In Ezekiel's prophecy God promised that this would all change back to His original intentions. What exactly would happen...? This is what Ezekiel told the land:

"'...But you, mountains of Israel, will produce branches and fruit...'" (v. 8)

"'...you will be plowed and sown...'" (v. 9)

"'The towns will be inhabited and the ruins rebuilt.'" (v. 10)

"'I will increase the number of people and animals living on you, and they will be fruitful and become numerous.'" (v. 11)

"'I will settle people on you as in the past and will make you prosper more than before.'" (v. 11)

This prophecy promised a physical and tangible restoration to the land, from a desolate wasteland to a lush and productive region, that would provide all that is needed for both man and animals. Yet, land does not simply produce by itself. It needs a people to plant it, to cultivate and care for it. However, this is not just any land, nor would these changes take place with just any people. Practical steps by a specific people were needed to bring about the fulfilment of Ezekiel's words spoken over the land.

WHEN WILL THIS CHANGE HAPPEN?

This prophecy is not a general or arbitrary encouragement, but a promise with a specific time frame. For the skeptical, if a prophecy does not describe its tangible fulfillment or include guidelines, what good is it? Hearing about a potential miraculous change is great, but many want to know "when will these things happen" or what will be the tipping point that begins this process? The answer seemed as unlikely in the early 1900s as it did to Ezekiel's hearers.

"'But you, mountains of Israel, will produce branches and fruit for **my people Israel**, for they will soon come home.'" (v. 8)

"'...and I will cause many people to live on you—**yes, all of Israel**. The towns will be inhabited and the ruins rebuilt.'" (v. 10)

"'I will cause people, **my people Israel**, to live on you. They will possess you, and you will be their inheritance.'" (v. 12)

This prophecy states that when Israel returns to this land, the land will produce fruit again, the Jewish population will multiply, and the desolate places will be rebuilt and inhabited. Yet, verse 12 states the real tipping point. This physical change will only happen when the land becomes Israel's possession and their inheritance once again. In other words, this prophecy states that the physical land will respond to Jewish independence and sovereignty over the region that was promised to their forefathers as an everlasting possession.

If these things could tangibly happen as foretold, it would be undeniable proof that such a dramatic natural change could only be seen as something "supernatural," or an act of God. This brings us to our final question, "Why would God want to transform a land and a people?" Let's consider this after we review the historical accounts, the photo comparisons, and the fact that it was all foretold two millennia ago.

THE HISTORY OF THE LAND

After spending some time clarifying some parameters in Ezekiel's prophecy, I moved on to the history of the region. I wanted to know "Is there any time in history that this could have been fulfilled?"

It has been over 2600 years since the time that Ezekiel spoke these words to the land of Israel. If we take an objective look at this ancient prophecy, we must consider if there is any other time in history that this could have come to pass. Let's review the many historical and eyewitness accounts of the land from Ezekiel's time until now. To follow Ezekiel's prophetic parameters, our timeline will give special attention to the land, agriculture, and times of Israeli/Jewish sovereignty. We will also note the invention of the modern camera in this process. At that point, we can begin to see for ourselves the same land that has been chronicled throughout the centuries by eyewitnesses and decide whether or not their accounts were accurate.

YEAR	PERIOD	LAND NAME	EYEWITNESS ACCOUNTS OF THE LAND
	Under Foreign Rule		
597–539 BCE	Time of Ezekiel; Babylon	Judea	
537–332 BCE	Return of Exiles; Second Temple	Judea	Ezra, Nehemiah
332–140 BCE	Greek Conquest	Judah	1 Macabees 1:29–39
	Jewish Independence		
140–63 BCE	Hasmonean Kingdom	Judah	1 Macabees 14:5–12
	Under Foreign Rule		
63–37 BCE	Roman Rule	Judah	
38–6 BCE	Roman Rule/Herod	Judah	
7BEC–AD 70	Roman Rule/Procurators	Judah	Flavius Josephus
71–306	Roman Rule/Explusion	Palestine	Dio Cassius
307–614	Byzantine Empire	Palestine	Helena; Paula
615–638	Persian Empire	Palestine	Patriarch of Jerusalem
639–1099	Multiple Moslem/Arab Rule	Palestine	Carl Voss; Baladhuri; Muqaddasi
1100–1291	Crusader Rule	Palestine	William of Tyre
1292–1516	Mameluks Rule	Palestine	Webbe; De Haas
1517–1917	Ottoman Empire	Palestine	various
1918–1948	British Mandate	Palestine	various
	Jewish Independence		
1948–Present	Israeli	Israel	

6th CENTURY BC

In approximately 597 BC, the Babylonians conquered Judea and carried away many of the residents of Jerusalem and surrounding cities as captives to the Babylonian empire. It is believed that after Ezekiel had been living for several years in Babylon that God began speaking to him through visions and experiences.

5th CENTURY BC

In the book of Nehemiah, the prophet first visits Jerusalem after seventy years of exile, with the permission of the Persian king Artaxerxes I. He described the city as lying "in ruins and its gates [having] been destroyed by fire?" Nehemiah said, "You see the bad situation we are in: Jerusalem is desolate and its gates have been destroyed by fire" (Nehemiah 2:3, 17). This stirred many Jews to return to the land and rebuild the walls of Jerusalem and the Temple in the time of Ezra and Nehemiah, while the city was still under Persian control.

3rd CENTURY BC
(Greek conquest and rule)

After the Babylonian rule of the region came the Greeks, who sought to establish Greek culture and religious influence in Jerusalem. This was accomplished through their deceitful conquest.

> "...the king sent the Mysian commander to the cities of Judah, and he came to Jerusalem with a strong force. He spoke to them deceitfully in peaceful terms, and they believed him. Then he attacked the city suddenly, in a great onslaught, and destroyed many of the people in Israel. He plundered the city and set fire to it, demolished its houses and its surrounding walls. And they took captive the women and children, and seized the animals...

> "They shed innocent blood around the sanctuary; they defiled the sanctuary. Because of them the inhabitants of Jerusalem fled away, she became the abode of strangers. She became a stranger to her own offspring, and her children forsook her. Her sanctuary became desolate as a wilderness..." (1st Macabees 1:29–39)

This led to the rise of the Macabean revolt, led by Judas Macabee, who eventually defeated and expelled the Greek armies and their influence. This victory brought about the Temple rededication that is still celebrated today as the feast of Hanukkah. This victory ushered in an eighty-year period of Jewish independence in the land.

2nd CENTURY BC
(Hasmonean rule – Jewish Independence)

Years after Judas' death, his brother, Simon Macabeeus, established the ruling dynasty in the land of Judea. From the account in 1 Macabees 14:4–12, the people and the land prospered under Jewish sovereignty.

> "The land was at rest all the days of Simon, who sought the good of his nation. His rule delighted his people and his glory all his days. As his crowning glory he took Joppa for a port and made it a gateway to the isles of the sea. He enlarged the borders of his nation and gained control of the countrys...

> "The people cultivated their land in peace; the land yielded its produce, the trees of the field their fruit. Old men sat in the squares, all talking about the good times, while the young men put on the glorious raiment of war. He supplied the cities with food and equipped them with means of defense, till his glorious name reached the ends of the earth. He brought peace to the land, and Israel was filled with great joy. Every one sat under his vine and fig tree, with no one to disturb them."

Throughout my research for quotes of eyewitness accounts of the land, this was the only example of recognizable prosperity that I could find in the last 2600 years. Ironically, it is under Jewish sovereignty.

1st CENTURY AD (Roman Empire)

Jewish rule did not last long before the Romans entered. Tensions were high for many years with violence and pockets of revolt springing up. This boiled over in AD 70 when the Romans laid siege to Jerusalem and eventually destroyed the Temple. This is an eyewitness account of what happened to the land during the siege:

> *"And now the Romans, although they were greatly distressed in getting together their materials, raised their banks in one and twenty days, after they had cut down all the trees that were in the country that adjoined to the city, and that for ninety furlongs [11 miles; 17.7 km] round about [Jerusalem], as I have already related. And truly the very view itself of the country was a melancholy thing; for those places which were before adorned with trees and pleasant gardens were now become a desolate country every way, and its trees were all cut down: nor could any foreigner that had formerly seen Judea and the most beautiful suburbs of the city, and now saw it as a desert, but lament and mourn sadly at so great a change: for the war had laid all the signs of beauty quite waste: nor if any one that had known the place before, had come on a sudden to it now, would he have known it again; but though he were at the city itself, yet would he have inquired for it notwithstanding."* (Josephus, 75 C.E.)

2nd CENTURY (Roman Empire)

After the Temple's destruction, revolts continued to spring up, which led to a crushing Roman response. The following is a Roman historian's account of what happened to Judah during the Bar Kochba revolt in AD 134.

> *"Of their forts the fifty strongest were razed to the ground. Nine hundred and eighty-five of their best-known villages were destroyed. ...*
>
> *"Thus the whole of Judea became desert, as indeed had been foretold to the Jews before the war. For the tomb of Solomon, whom these folk celebrate in their sacred rites, fell of its own accord into fragments, and wolves and hyenas, many in number, roamed howling through their cities."* (Cassius Dio, 4)

It was common for the Roman Empire to change the names of conquered land, as we will see in some of our photo descriptions. As a result of this long, costly, and frustrating conflict, Emperor Hadrian changed the name of the region to Syria Palaestina, naming the land after ancient Israel's archenemies, the Philistines, in an attempt to remove any Jewish identity or link to the land. From this time until 1948, the region was often referred to as "Palestine."

The next 1800 years were a progression of wars and desolation that were truly devastating to the land. For more historical eyewitness accounts of Jews, Christians, and Muslims from multiple empires who recorded what they saw and experienced in this region, please find Reference #1 in the back of this book. For our purposes, we will jump ahead to the mid-1800s to two major events that have shaped much of our view of the land in this time: the invention of the modern camera and Mark Twain's travel journals through this land in 1867 that were recorded in his book *The Innocents Abroad*.

CAMERA OBSCURA

Around 1820, the invention of the modern camera—or "camera obscura"—changed the world forever. While the concept of light passing through a small hole and projecting an inverted image of the scene in front of the camera had been around for centuries, it was now made into something more mobile and "user friendly." Thanks to just a few of the adventurous pioneers listed here, we have some of the first ever photos of the Holy Land starting in the mid-1800s.

- Joseph-Philibert Girault de Prangey studied painting in Paris. He was keenly interested in the architecture of the Middle East, and he toured Italy and the countries of the eastern Mediterranean between 1841 and 1844, producing over 900 daguerreotypes of architectural views, landscapes, and portraits. He is credited with taking the first ever photos of Jerusalem in 1844, seen below (www.smithsonianmag.com; "See the first photographs ever taken of Jerusalem" by Rose Eveleth, Jan 23, 2014).

- In 1855 Francis Frith sold his holdings in a successful grocery store and cutlery business, and started a photography studio. By 1856 he felt sufficiently competent to take the cumbersome equipment required on his first tour of Egypt and Palestine in 1856–7, where the heat and strong light drove him to develop the negatives in tombs, temples, and caves. His pictures of the Sphinx, the pyramids, and other scenes from Egypt and the Holy Land made him a legend. (Todd Gustavson, *Camera: A History of Photography,* Sterling Publishing Co, 2009, p. 38; www.francisfrith.com/us/pages/frith-biography)

- By the late 1800s, several photographers connected to the American Colony in Jerusalem were also combing the region, capturing local portraits, culture, biblical locations, and accompanying western expeditions. The photo collections of the American Colony represent some of the best photo collections available from that time period and consist of the majority of the photo recreations used in this book.

Egyptian views; The pyramids of Gizeh. Photographer [Lewis Larsson] near top of Great Pyramid; Date: 1900–1905

Jamil Albina with a film dryer at the American Colony; Date: 1898–1930

Perhaps most importantly, the invention of the "camera obscura" validates the chronicles of almost 2000 years of eyewitness accounts of the region. We are able to see the effects of the oppressive Ottoman Empire that ruled for another seventy years after the first photos of Jerusalem were taken. It also gives a stark visual into the region and era that Mark Twain experienced and wrote of in his travel journal covering his 1867 tour of the Holy Land. By the time Mark Twain arrived, some of these adventure photographers had been capturing photographs of the region for twenty years.

THE ANCIENT PROPHECY | 17

MARK TWAIN

Mark Twain visited the Holy Land in 1867 and published his impressions in *The Innocents Abroad*. His writings have impacted millions of people since then and are some of the most well-known comments about the region from that era. He described a desolate country, devoid of both vegetation and human population throughout his journey as he rode from Damascus to Jerusalem, then on to Jaffa on the coast. The following are excerpts of what he saw along the way, then later recorded in the wit that he was known for.

While riding in what is now the northern edge Israel:

Here were evidences of cultivation—a rare sight in this country—an acre or two of rich soil studded with last season's dead corn-stalks of the thickness of your thumb and very wide apart. But in such a land it was a thrilling spectacle. Close to it was a stream, and on its banks a great herd of curious-looking Syrian goats and sheep were gratefully eating gravel. I do not state this as a petrified fact—I only suppose they were eating gravel, because there did not appear to be anything else for them to eat.

There is not a solitary village throughout its whole extent—not for thirty miles in either direction. There are two or three small clusters of Bedouin tents, but not a single permanent habitation. One may ride ten miles, hereabouts, and not see ten human beings.

It is seven in the morning, and as we are in the country, the grass ought to be sparkling with dew, the flowers enriching the air with their fragrance, and the birds singing in the trees. But alas, there is no dew here, nor flowers, nor birds, nor trees. There is a plain and an unshaded lake, and beyond them some barren mountains. (Chapter 46)

His first impressions of the Galilee region:

It is solitude, for birds and squirrels on the shore and fishes in the water are all the creatures that are near to make it otherwise, but it is not the sort of solitude to make one dreary. Come to Galilee for that. If these unpeopled deserts, these rusty mounds of barrenness, that never, never, never do shake the glare from their harsh outlines, and fade and faint into vague perspective… (Chapter 48)

While riding south from the Galilee, through the biblical heartland towards Jerusalem:

The further we went the hotter the sun got, and the more rocky and bare, repulsive and dreary the landscape became. There could not have been more fragments of stone strewn broadcast over this part of the world, if every ten square feet of the land had been occupied by a separate and distinct stonecutter's establishment for an age. There was hardly a tree or a shrub anywhere. Even the olive and the cactus, those fast friends of a worthless soil, had almost deserted the country. No landscape exists that is more tiresome to the eye than that which bounds the approaches to Jerusalem. The only difference between the roads and the surrounding country, perhaps, is that there are rather more rocks in the roads than in the surrounding country. (Chapter 52)

Trying to describe what he saw upon arriving in Jerusalem:

A fast walker could go outside the walls of Jerusalem and walk entirely around the city in an hour. I do not know how else to make one understand how small it is. The appearance of the city is peculiar. It is as knobby with countless little domes as a prison door is with bolt-heads. (Chapter 53)

After visiting the Dead Sea:

The desert and the barren hills gleam painfully in the sun, around the Dead Sea, and there is no pleasant thing or living creature upon it or about its borders to cheer the eye. It is a scorching, arid, repulsive solitude. A silence broods over the scene that is depressing to the spirits. It makes one think of funerals and death. (Chapter 55)

By the time Mark Twain had reached Jaffa, he was exhausted by his travels, seemingly stunned by what he saw and ready for the journey to end as he boarded his ship. As he recorded his parting thoughts in a way only Mark Twain could, he let his readers know exactly what his overall thoughts were of the Holy Land:

Of all the lands there are for dismal scenery, I think Palestine must be the prince. The hills are barren, they are dull of color, they are unpicturesque in shape. The valleys are unsightly deserts fringed with a feeble vegetation that has an expression about it of being sorrowful and despondent. The Dead Sea and the Sea of Galilee sleep in the midst of a vast stretch of hill and plain wherein the eye rests upon no pleasant tint, no striking object, no soft picture dreaming in a purple haze or mottled with the shadows of the clouds. Every outline is harsh, every feature is distinct, there is no perspective—distance works no enchantment here. It is a hopeless, dreary, heart-broken land.

Palestine sits in sackcloth and ashes. Over it broods the spell of a curse that has withered its fields and fettered its energies. Where Sodom and Gomorrah reared their domes and towers, that solemn sea now floods the plain, in whose bitter waters no living thing exists—over whose waveless surface the blistering air hangs motionless and dead—about whose borders nothing grows but weeds, and scattering tufts of cane, and that treacherous fruit that promises refreshment to parching lips, but turns to ashes at the touch. Nazareth is forlorn; about that ford of Jordan where the hosts of Israel entered the Promised Land with songs of rejoicing, one finds only a squalid camp of fantastic Bedouins of the desert; Jericho the accursed, lies a moldering ruin, to-day, even as Joshua's miracle left it more than three thousand years ago; Bethlehem and Bethany, in their poverty and their humiliation, have nothing about them now to remind one that they once knew the high honor of the Saviour's presence; the hallowed spot where the shepherds watched their flocks by night, and where the angels sang Peace on earth, good will to men, is untenanted by any living creature, and unblessed by any feature that is pleasant to the eye. Renowned Jerusalem itself, the stateliest name in history, has lost all its ancient grandeur, and is become a pauper village; the riches of Solomon are no longer there to compel the admiration of visiting Oriental queens; the wonderful temple which was the pride and the glory of Israel, is gone, and the Ottoman crescent is lifted above the spot where, on that most memorable day in the annals of the world, they reared the Holy Cross. The noted Sea of Galilee, where Roman fleets once rode at anchor and the disciples of the Saviour sailed in their ships, was long ago deserted by the devotees of war and commerce, and its borders are a silent wilderness; Capernaum is a shapeless ruin; Magdala is the home of beggared Arabs; Bethsaida and Chorazin have vanished from the earth, and the "desert places" round about them where thousands of men once listened to the Saviour's voice and ate the miraculous bread, sleep in the hush of a solitude that is inhabited only by birds of prey and skulking foxes.

Palestine is desolate and unlovely. And why should it be otherwise? Can the curse of the Deity beautify a land?

Palestine is no more of this work-day world. It is sacred to poetry and tradition—it is dream-land. (chapter 56)

Less than eighty years after Mark Twain's dismal journals, everything he described began changing. He could have never dreamed that the same desolate and unforgiving land that he struggled through and wrote of is the same land that is prospering as an agricultural and technological powerhouse today. Unfortunately, he never saw that change because he passed away in 1910. Even then in the early twentieth century, the "curse" that he wrote about seemed to continue.

20TH CENTURY
(Ottoman Empire/British Mandate/ Israel)

As the land entered the twentieth century, still under the Ottoman Empire, it seemed that the desolation continued:

> *"There was a severe outbreak of typhus and in 1915 a plague of locusts 'fell from the sky as thick as snowflakes in a Scandinavian storm' and stripped the country bare, bringing the population to the point of starvation."*
>
> (*American Colony History Brochure,* Jerusalem, 2008, p. 13)

After the British victory in Palestine in World War I, British and American developers flooded the region by the 1930s, looking to improve the quality of life. This is what they found:

> *"We found it inhabited by fellahin who lived in mud hovels and suffered severely from the prevalent malaria.... Large areas ... were uncultivated...."* (Lewis French, the British Director of Development writing of Palestine in, *The Hope-Simpson Report* [London, 1930], www.jewishvirtuallibrary.org/jsource/History/Hope_Simpson.html)

Walter Lowdermilk, representative of the U.S. Soil Conservation Service, traveled to the Middle East in 1938–39. He described the land in biblical times as having rich red earth and forested hillsides. He wrote that this hillsides were stripped of their topsoil when desert Arabs cut down the trees, leaving the country *"...a desert land with no one to till the soil..."* He declared that *"the decay of Palestine reached its darkest stage in the four hundred years of Turkish rule, from 1517 to 1918."* (Lowdermilk, *Palestine: Land of Promise*, pp. 5, 74–76)

MAY 14, 1948 to PRESENT (Israel)

When Israeli sovereignty took over in 1948, stunning changes became evident throughout the land in comparison to the previous 2000 years.

> *"Since Israel attained its independence in 1948–2002, the total area under cultivation has increased from 165,000 ha. to some 420,000 ha., and the number of agricultural communities has grown from 400 to 900 (including 136 Arab villages)."* (Israel ministry of Foreign affairs, article: *Israel's Agriculture in the 21st Century* by Jon Fedler, 2002)

> *"Since the establishment of the state of Israel in 1948, agricultural output has increased twelve-fold, while water usage only three-fold."* (2011 Israel's Agriculture booklet; Ministry of Agriculture and Rural Development, p. 18)

> *After 10 years of existence, Israel "had more than doubled its cultivated land, to a million acres. It had drained 44,000 acres of marshland and extended irrigation to 325,000 acres . . . On vast stretches of uncultivable land it had established new range-cover to support a growing livestock industry and planted 37 million trees in new forests and shelter belts."* ("The Reclamation of a Man-Made Desert," *The Scientific American*, April, 1960)

> *"Israel is the only country in the world where the desert is receding, and a pre-conference statement from the U.N. Development Programme called the Jewish state 'one of the driest, but agriculturally most successful, countries of the world. Israel's knowledge of drylands agriculture could be of great value to some of the world's poorest people."* (American Associates Ben Gurion University of the Negev, August 8, 2008 Article: "In the Desert: Why Israel Is a Model for Some of the World's Driest Countries")

> In Israel, *"more than 80 percent of household waste water is recycled, amounting to 400 million cubic meters a year, the Environment Ministry says. That ratio is four times higher than in any other country, according to Israel's water authority."* (Reuters, Nov 14, 2010; "Arid Israel recycles waste water on a grand scale" by Ari Rabinovitch.)

With its world leadership in water irrigation drip technology, water recycling, and water desalinization plants, it was reported in 2015 that *"Israel exports $2.2 billion annually in water-related tech and know-how."* (TimesofIsrael.com; "How Israel became a water superpower," by Simona Weinglass, December 1, 2015)

"Israeli technology has made the country's 'Super Cows' world famous, as they produce much more milk than other countries' cows, up to 10.5 tons a year, 10% more than in the U.S. and almost 50% more than in Germany... The Bible, no less, describes Israel as a land flowing with milk and honey. In that respect, it's been proven at least half-right: Israel has by far the most productive dairy cows in the world." ("The Land of Milk: Israel's Super Cows Are the World's Most Productive" by Joshua Levitt *The Algemeiner*, March 11, 2014, quoting a report on Bloomberg News report, March 11, 2014, "The Super Cows Making Israel Flow with Milk," by Elliott Gotkine)

While there could be positive and negatives found in every century regarding the land's agriculture, population, and conflicts, the overwhelming information is stunning. Perhaps even more stunning are the dramatic changes since 1948, occurring during Israel's multiple regional wars, conflicts, and streams of violence. The only noticeable catalyst in this change was that the Jews had begun returning to their homeland and regained national sovereignty for the first time in 2000 years, just as Ezekiel had prophesied.

As we've seen, the land had been occupied by a succession of invaders and conquerors, becoming more of an eroded wasteland as time crept on. Throughout those conquests, the land seemed to reject every other national sovereignty and wait for Israel's return. The land never became a homeland for any other group, nor would the land thrive and fully produce for any others. As recorded by these eyewitnesses, prior to 1948 much of the Holy Land remained a barren, desolate, insect, and disease-filled ruin regardless of who ruled it.

It could be argued that God, the Jewish people, and the land seem to form a holy triangle of sorts. As history demonstrates, when one of those elements was removed, nothing worked. In biblical times, when the people forgot God, or overworked the land, it led to their expulsion. When the people were out of the land, the land lay desolate and barren, while the people cried out to God and longed to return to it. Now that God is bringing His people back to the land, the land is responding in the most fruitful way it ever has—for the people it was intended for. It was as if the land and its people were two long-lost lovers, faithful to each other and waiting to be together again.

The first command Ezekiel speaks to the land was to the trees to "put forth your branches": *"'But you, mountains of Israel, will produce branches and fruit for my people Israel, for they will soon come home....'"* (Ezekiel 36:8) Ironically, this is exactly how the changes began in the early 1900s when the Jewish National Fund began planting trees in Palestine that had been decimated by the Ottoman taxation of trees. "JNF has planted more than 240 million trees in Israel, providing luscious belts of green covering more than 250,000 acres." (https://secure.jnf.org/site/Donation2?df_id=6827&6827.donation=form1) The JNF planted trees, groves, and entire forests in areas long since cut down as well as in areas where they had never grown before. Soon erosion was reduced, animal life emerged, fragile ecosystems were strengthened, and weather patterns soon were affected over the region. And "My people Israel" came...as they still are doing today. Today the JNF website reports that Israel is one of only two countries in the world that entered the 21st century with a net gain in its number of trees.

Reading the personal accounts throughout the centuries provides a stark contrast from the land that we know today. Was it really that drastic and barren, or were the writers back then simply taking poetic license or embellishing the truth? Was it just a small area that was desolate, or was it true for the entire region? Thanks to the photographers in the mid to late 1800s that traveled throughout the Holy Land, we can have a look for ourselves and compare it with today.

THE ANCIENT PROPHECY | 21

The Modern Lens
THE PHOTOS

I love the old black-and-white photos from the Holy Land. I could wander aimlessly through Jerusalem's old city, visiting the photo shops that are off the beaten path, just to flip through all the old photo collections. I often have a sense of awe when I discover a new angle of the land that I haven't seen before and marvel at how much has changed in a short 70–100 years.

Most of the black-and-white photos in this book, including the title descriptions and photo dates, are from "The American Colony: Eric Mattson Collection," unless otherwise noted. The American Colony has done the world a true service by cataloging, restoring, and digitizing their collection. It's one of the best preserved and extensive collections available from the 1880–1950. All of our modern photos were captured and edited during the summer and fall of 2016, by Elise Monique Photography. During these six weeks of photo shoots, I often felt like an excited and giddy child on a treasure hunt to find the exact spot where these old photos were originally taken. The searches were a lot of fun with unexpected people, adventures, and stories to go with them. You'll find these stories scattered throughout the book under the heading "Personal Encounters and beside the photos that created the setting for each "personal encounter."

As stated earlier, whenever possible, the exact angle and location of the original photographs were sought out to recreate our modern-day photos. In several locations, due to the dramatic growth of the population, cities, and agriculture, this was often impossible, so we settled with as close as we could get. Ironically, these unexpected and momentary frustrations due to our inability to recreate photos from only eighty years ago simply demonstrated the goal of this project—to visually show this land's dramatic and accelerated changes in such a short amount of time, compared with the much longer periods of desolation during many of the years since Ezekiel foretold these changes 2600 years ago. I hope you enjoy the locations and photo comparisons as much as I enjoyed seeking them out.

GALILEE AND GOLAN

> *By the end of the 18th century, the great forests of the Galilee and the Carmel mountain range were denude of trees; swamps and deserts encroached on agricultural land. Palestine was truly a poor, neglected, no-man's land with no important cities."*
>
> (Clarence Wagner, "365 Fascinating facts about Israel," #311, C-2006)

Migdal (believed to be the ancient town of Magdala until 2009, when archeology proved otherwise) is found on the northwest side of the lake. Modern Tiberias can be seen on the distant ridge in the 2016 photo.

Magdala (Migdal) from the North; Date: 1910–1920

PERSONAL ENCOUNTERS:
The Land Is Calling

On a ridiculously hot and humid day in May, I found a little café on the north side of Lake Kinneret to escape the heat. The manager, Ori, had just made some amazing cherry jam using cherries from the Arab farmer across the road. There are many places throughout Israel where Arabs and Jews not only work together, but are friends and help one another out. This is just one of the many examples that no one seems to hear about.

It was well after the lunch rush and business was slow enough for Ori to join us. We heard his story about growing up on the north side of the Galilee, but he had

Magdala (Migdal) from the North; Date: 2016

also lived in Australia, Thailand, Canada, and elsewhere. Yet, after several years, he recently returned home to Israel to build his home overlooking the sea. Like many Israelis, he travelled and worked overseas, but something within him seems to have pulled him home to this land. When he had the opportunity to take over a café close to his childhood home, he took it. While he didn't seem to be a religious man, I was struck by his sincerity and devotion to the land. Many Jews from around the world, like him, are hearing the same call in their hearts, saying, "It's time to come home to the land."

> *…Magdala is not a beautiful place …is the home of beggared Arabs…"*
> (Mark Twain, *Innocents Abroad*, 1867, Chapter 48, 56)

Pillars at Hazor looking east over the Hula Valley; Date: 1898–1946;

HAZOR

According to Joshua chapter 11, Hazor was the capital city of the Canaanite inhabitants, which was destroyed and burned by Joshua. Later Jeremiah prophesied,

*Hazor excavations;
Date: 2016*

❝ *Hazor will become a haunt of jackals, a desolate place forever. No one will live there; no people will dwell in it."*

(Jeremiah 49:33)

Huleh Valley and Mount Hermon; Date: 1934–1939

HULA BASIN

The Hula valley is about thirty minutes north of the Sea of Galilee in Northern Israel. Since the Roman conquest in the first century, this one fertile and thickly populated region became a malarial infested swampy marsh. Today, due to the work of Jewish pioneers this vast valley has become some of the most fertile farmland in all of Israel, full of fields, orchards, groves, vineyards, and growing communities.

*Hula Valley, Mount Hermon and the town of Rosh Pina;
Date: 2016*

> *In Roman times and before, this region was fertile and thickly populated, but it had become a dismal swamp and a focus of malarial infection to the country at large. Sediments from the uplands to the north had progressively filled in the northern end of Lake Huleh, thus creating a marsh that was overgrown with papyrus. The marshes have now been drained by widening and deepening the mouth of the lake to bring down its water level and by a system of drainage canals. The Huleh Reclamation Authority estimates that this little Garden of Eden will support a population of 100,000 in an intensive agricultural economy, cultivating vegetables, grapes, fruits, peanuts, grains, sugar cane, rice—even fish (in ponds impounded on the old lake bed).*

("The Reclamation of a Man-Made Desert," *Scientific American,* April, 1960)

Huleh lake reserve;
Date: 1910–1920

Huleh lake reserve;
Date: 2016

Nazareth from the East, bridle path in foreground; Date: 1898–1946

NAZARETH

Nazareth was the childhood home of Jesus. At that time, this small town had an estimated 400 people; today it boasts over 75,000.

> **The crowds answered, "This is Jesus, the prophet from Nazareth in Galilee."**
>
> (Matthew 21:11)

Nazareth from the East, Date: 2016

> *17th century "…an inconsiderable village [Nazareth] …nothing here but a vast and spacious ruin."*
>
> (Henry Maundrell, *The Journal of Henry Maundrell from Aleppo to Jerusalem*, 1697, Bohn's edition (London, 1848), respectively pp. 477, 428, 450)

THE MODERN LENS

*Nazareth from the east;
Date: 1894*

*Jezreel Valley from
the Nazareth hills;
Date: 1898–1946*

*Nazareth from the east;
Date: 2016*

*Jezreel Valley from
the Nazareth hills;
Date: 2016*

The Jezreel Valley from Nazareth;
Date: 1910–1920

The Jezreel Valley from Nazareth;
Date: 2016

*Subeibeh, Nimrod's Fortress;
Date: 1910–1920*

NIMROD'S FORTRESS

While not mentioned in the Bible, this castle dates back to crusader battles of the thirteenth century. The stunning aspect is not the actual castle, but the growth of trees and vegetation since the original photo.

*Subeibeh, Nimrod's Fortress;
Date: 2016*

*Sea of Galilee southern end from the East;
Date: 1934–1939*

SEA OF GALILEE

In 1867 Charles Wyllys Elliott, president of Harvard University, wrote:

Sea of Galilee southern end from the East; Date: 2016

> " *A beautiful sea lies unbosomed among the Galilean hills, in the midst of that land once possessed by Zebulon and Naphtali, Asher and Dan… Life here was once idyllic, charming…It was a world of ease, simplicity, and beauty; now it is a scene of desolation and misery."*
>
> (Charles Wyllys Elliott, *Remarkable Characters and Places of the Holy Land*, Hartford, Connecticut: J.B. Burr & Company, 1867)

Ein Gev Pier;
Date: October 1945

Ein Gev is a kibbutz on the east side of the lake, established in 1937.

Hippos (Susita) summit with sea and Tiberias;
Date: 1934–1939

Hippos, sometimes called Susita, was one of the ten city-states of the Roman Decapolis in the first century, found on a plateau on the eastern side of the lake. This town has New Testament connections and is mentioned in the Talmud. The town seen in the distance on the other side is Tiberias.

Ein Gev Pier;
Date: 2016

Hippos (Susita) excavations and modern Tiberias in the distance:
Date: 2016

The ruins here are of a fourth-century synagogue built upon the ruins of a first-century synagogue that Jesus taught in as mentioned in the New Testament.

*Capernaum Synagogue;
Date: 1920–1933*

CAPERNAUM

In Hebrew Capernaum is pronounced "Kafar-nahum," or "village of Nahum." While not much is known, it is believed by some to be the town of Nahum the prophet.

> *Leaving Nazareth, he went and lived in Capernaum, which was by the lake in the area of Zebulun and Naphtali—"*
>
> (Matthew 4:13)

Capernaum Synagogue;
Date: 2016

> *Capernaum was only a shapeless ruin. It bore no semblance to a town, and had nothing about it to suggest that it had ever been a town."*
>
> (Mark Twain, *Innocents Abroad*)

Capernaum, remains of the western Synagogue wall;
Date: 1910–1920

Capernaum, western Synagogue wall;
Date: 2016

Tiberias, aeriel view from 1000 meters altitude; Date: 1909–1910

TIBERIAS

Located on the west side of the sea, Tiberias was founded in AD 18 by Herod Antipas and named after Emperor Tiberias Caesar. It is revered as one of the four holy cities of Judaism and became the religious, cultural, and administrative capital after the fall of Jerusalem. Christians will find it mentioned a few times in the New Testament as a location Jesus interacted with.

> *Then some boats from Tiberias landed near the place where the people had eaten the bread after the Lord had given thanks."* (John 6:23)

Tiberias, aeriel view from 1000 meters altitude;
Date: 2016

> **To find the sort of solitude to make one dreary one must come to Galilee for that... this stupid village of Tiberias, slumbering under its six funereal palms...."**
> (Mark Twain, *The Innocents Abroad*, pp. 366, 375)

Tiberias lakefront;
Date: 1940–1946

PERSONAL ENCOUNTERS:
The Juice Man

Ya'acov has been Tiberias' juice man since his mother bought him his first juicer as a young boy. "*I was given a lot of oranges, so my mother got me a juicer and told me 'make the people juice'. . . so I did and the people kept coming back,*" he shared in a thick Hebrew accent. He added more fruit and the business grew. After a couple visits (because it's THAT good and you can't beat cold fresh juice on a hot day), we just show up and he says, "*I make something for you with carrots, oranges, melon. . .*" I just nod my head and smile, knowing that whatever he concocts is always

Tiberias lakefront;
Date: 2016

amazing. After a few more visits, we have some time to sit with him. He takes out a guitar and passionately strums it, belting out a song in Spanish, something about love. I'm taken aback by the passion with which he shares his song. It is as if he is playing to thousands of adoring juice lovers. Not in a prideful way, just enveloped in a song he enjoys, playing in a land and to a people that he loves. It's contagious.

This land is so diverse, as are the people who live here. It's amazing to think that one hundred years ago, Tiberias was a run-down and forgotten village. Today it's coming back to life. This miracle can be seen through a man who makes juice from the land's bounty and turns it into a prospering local business.

JEZREEL VALLEY

The Jezreel Valley runs west to east just south of the Sea of Galilee and provides the setting for several biblical events. Until Jewish immigration in the 1920s, the Jezreel Valley had several large malarial infested swamps. At that time, the swamps were drained by hand and have since become known as the "breadbasket of Israel" and some of the richest farmland in all of Israel.

Ein Herod, new Settlement started in 1921; Date: May 26, 1935

EIN HEROD

Founded in 1921 in the Jerzeel Valley near Mt Gilboa, Ein Herod was one of Israel's first "green" kibbutz that introduced several environmental projects. Notice the replanted forests in the background of the new photo.

Ein Herod;
Date: 2016

> *In the vicinity of the biblical Mount Gilboa, 'as elsewhere, as everywhere in Palestine, city and palaces have returned to the dust; this melancholy of abandonment, weighs on all the Holy Land.'"*

(Pierre Loti, La Galilee (Paris, 1895), pp. 37-41, 69, 85-86, 69, cited by David Landes, "Palestine Before the Zionists," Commentary, February 1976, pp. 48-49.)

Aerial view of Gilboa and Ein Herod;
Date: 1932

Aerial view of Gilboa and Ein Herod;
Date: 2016

AFULA

With history dating back to the crusader era and beyond, modern Afula was founded in 1925 when the American Zionist Commonwealth purchased the area of the valley from the Sursuk family of Beirut. Today it lies in heart of the Jezreel Valley.

Afula settlement, founded in 1925; Date: 1925–1933

PERSONAL ENCOUNTERS:
The Warm Ray of Heavenly Sunlight

"*You have old pictures of Afula…?*" asked the municipality secretary. "*Why do you want pictures of here and not of nicer places…?* Most of this conversation came through a translator, because it was hard to find many English speakers in Afula. In fact, unless you are Israeli, you may have never heard of this place, as there is nothing of historical or biblical significance that happened there. She might have said, "Can anything good come out of Afula?"…just as someone once said about the neighboring town of Nazareth. Yet this is exactly why I was interested in these shots.

Afula;
Date: 2016

I wanted to recreate this shot. We found the old synagogue in this photo. We found the main street. We even found the location where this photo was taken…from the roof of an old four-story apartment building. Given our previous experiences with gaining access to apartment buildings, I think my exact words were: "Gaahh, we're definitely not getting that shot…it's residential." Just to be sure, I decided to confirm my doubts, so I slowly wandered into the building searching for the elevator to the top floor, expecting disappointment.

Disappointment never came. As the elevator doors opened to the top floor, my excitement rushed back as we stepped into the warm bright ray of almost heavenly sunlight. Directly in front of us stood a black iron ladder, leading to the roof, with its ceiling hatch already opened, as if waiting for us. I looked around to make sure no one was suspiciously scowling at me and climbed up to the roof. As I did, I smiled at the fact that I was completely wrong about my expectations and wondered about the municipality's reaction to the photo comparisons showing the growth of their town. Can anything good come from Afula? It most certainly can… and it has.

*Beth Shean from the South;
Date: 1921–1933*

BETH SHEAN

Dating back to the Canaanite period, Beth Shean is the location of King Saul's well-known demise at the hands of the Philistines mentioned in the Bible. During the Roman period, this site was known as Scythopolis, the leading city in the Decapolis. Today, Beth Shean is one of the largest archeological parks in Israel and is home to some of the most well-preserved Roman ruins in the region.

Beth Shean from the South;
Date: 2016

> *The next day, when the Philistines came to strip the dead, they found Saul and his three sons fallen on Mount Gilboa. ⁹ They cut off his head and stripped off his armor, and they sent messengers throughout the land of the Philistines to proclaim the news in the temple of their idols and among their people. ¹⁰ They put his armor in the temple of the Ashtoreths and fastened his body to the wall of Beth Shan."*
>
> (1 Samuel 31:8–10)

Beth Shean, Arab village of Beisan;
Date: 1898–1914

Beth Shean, Arab village of Beisan;
Date: 2016

Mount Tabor from the Jezreel Valley; Date: 1910–1920

MOUNT TABOR

In the heart of the Jezreel Valley, Mount Tabor is the site of the defeat of Sisera at the hands of Barak, as found in Judges, chapter 4. It is also the traditional site of the transfiguration of Jesus in the New Testament.

Mount Tabor from the Jezreel Valley; Date: 2016

" *When they told Sisera that Barak son of Abinoam had gone up to Mount Tabor...*"

(Judges 4:12)

" *We reached Tabor safely. . . . We never saw a human being on the whole route.*"

(Mark Twain, *The Innocents Abroad*, pp. 366, 375)

THE MODERN LENS | 65

*Mount Tabor;
Date: 1934–1939*

PERSONAL ENCOUNTERS:
The Steepest of Hills

If you took the veins and capillaries in the human body and then turned them into a map, you would have the layout of this town. No pattern, no rhyme or reason, no modern surveying techniques—just mostly paved roads (many one-way roads with no signs) surrounded by the dusty gray walls of concrete homes that barely allow for the width of a car, let alone for all the bikes, kids, and motorcycles that appear out of nowhere.

Undeterred, we were on the hunt for "the spot" of this photo, or as close as we could get. On the GPS, I could see a hard left-hand turn coming up that "should" get us close. As I slowly made a sharp left turn, making sure I wasn't scraping any part of the car or someone else's, I was rendered speechless from what I saw in front of us. It was the steepest "mostly" paved road I'd ever seen. Ever. So steep that I've wiped out attempting to snow ski down hills with *much* less of an incline. Yet there were

Mount Tabor;
Date: 2016

cars parked at odd angles near the top, so someone had driven up there. Not wanting to feel like a coward, I pressed forward and started the treacherous climb. In the car, it felt like the angle of an airplane's takeoff. The car's transmission started to smell like something was burning, and I began envisioning the transmission exploding, and then a sudden backwards free fall slide to whatever concrete lay below us. I looked over at our photographer, Elise, who was sitting in the passenger seat. Her eyes were wide, her arms bracing herself, and she was laughing nervously, trying to trust my judgment and driving skills as we ascended. I held the steering wheel in a death grip and tried to remember to breath.

After the longest and most tedious fifteen seconds of my life, we made it to "the top. But "top" suggests a level plateau. Instead, there was a beautiful Arab-style house on the same ridiculous incline with barely enough space to turn a car around or park while a driver fights gravity's attempt to pull himself from the driver's seat. I looked at the house and spotted two smiling women pointing from the window, enjoying the show of a determined young woman in a big navy blue hat and a large camera, , all but roll out of the car and find her footing on the incline. Soon another window opened, and a middle-aged man curiously asked in a thick Arab accent, "*Are you tourist?*" I'm pretty sure that was obvious.

Somehow, we conquered gravity and made it back to the "normal" spider-veined streets, but not before getting this shot from a town that wasn't there a hundred years ago. After finding a mouthwatering Arab bakery, a couple potent shots of Turkish coffee, and a plate of some warm hummus from a shop owner that didn't speak a lick of English, we moved on to the next town and the next adventure.

JUDEA AND SAMARIA

One of my favorite places in all of Israel is Judea and Samaria. This region is where 80% of the Bible happened. Unfortunately, due to the current political climate, many Israeli simply don't go because of safety concerns. Many Israelis have never seen the photos in this section, let alone traveled there, though it's less than a forty-five-minute drive from several major cities. It is my pleasure to share these photos as well as my experience in taking them, which was far less harrowing than one would think.

As we look at the biblical heartland of Judea and Samaria, sometimes called the West Bank, we find several biblical towns that currently fall under the Palestinian Authority's security and civil control, referred to as "Area A" under the Oslo Accords. While some of these towns have large Arab populations, and the Israeli government restricts Jews from living there due to security concerns, they are still technically under Israeli national influence. This fact alone has brought about dramatic positive changes for the Arab population in this region, as opposed to what they experienced under Jordanian rule prior to 1967. While the living standards are not as high as in

Jewish communities, or "Israel proper," it is comparably higher than the surrounding Arab nations. Consider the following data:

"During the 1970s, the West Bank and Gaza constituted the fourth fastest-growing economy in the world—ahead of such 'wonders' as Singapore, Hong Kong, and Korea, and substantially ahead of Israel itself.... Under Israeli rule, the Palestinians also made vast progress in social welfare. Perhaps most significantly, mortality rates in the West Bank and Gaza fell by more than two-thirds between 1970 and 1990, while life expectancy rose from 48 years in 1967 to 72 in 2000 (compared with an average of 68 years for all the countries of the Middle East and North Africa.)....By 1986, 92.8 percent of the population in the West Bank and Gaza had electricity around the clock, as compared to 20.5 percent in 1967; 85 percent had running water in dwellings, as compared to 16 percent in 1967; 83.5 percent had electric or gas ranges for cooking, as compared to 4 percent in 1967; and so on for refrigerators, televisions, and cars." (Efriam Karsh, *Arafat's War*, New York: Grove Press 2003*)*

Bethlehem from the Southeast; Date: 1934–1939

BETHLEHEM

In the shadow of Jerusalem, Bethlehem quietly sits only five miles away. From the burial place of Rachel, to the romance of Boaz and Ruth, to the young David shepherding his flocks, to the birthplace of Jesus, this small biblical town is mentioned throughout the Bible starting in Genesis.

Bethlehem from the Southeast;
Date: 2016

❝ *So Rachel died and was buried on the way to Ephrath (that is, Bethlehem)."*

(Genesis 35:19)

❝ *(1867) Bethlehem and Bethany, in their poverty and their humiliation, have nothing about them now to remind one that they once knew the high honor of the Savior's presence; the hallowed spot where the shepherds watched their flocks by night, and where the angels sang, 'Peace on earth, good will to men,' is untenanted by any living creature…"*

(Mark Twain, Chapter 56)

Bethlehem and the Herodian in the distance; Date: 1934–1939

PERSONAL ENCOUNTERS:
Slow Visits, Fast Work

I have a friend who loves fast motorcycles and has a history of outrunning police in foreign countries. He enjoys heavy metal music, plays a mean hand of poker, and is constantly smiling as he tells of countless adventures. When we're together, he's shockingly generous, would give you the shirt off his back, and is a joy to be around. One might think this describes a young movie star, with the world at his fingertips. Yet, this is Ahmed, an older Palestinian Christian man living with his family in Bethlehem. There is no one better that I could choose to help us find some of these older photos of his town.

Bethlehem and the Herodian in the distance; Date: 2016

When we arrived to pick him up, I was quickly reminded that there is no such thing as a quick visit to his home. Soon the table was full of coffee, amazing salads, fruit, and breads while his lovely wife dismissed my heartfelt thanks with "*Oh, this is nothing.*" I knew she was right. I've been to their home for a planned meal. It is Arab hospitality fit for kings and unlike any I've experienced anywhere else in the world. It would be some time before we could even talk about leaving or finding the old photo locations.

When we finally set out, the momentary fears I had about lost time to find particular photo angles were unfounded. "*I think I know where this one is…*" he said with a wink and a dry smile. We parked nearby, walked through a security gate behind the hospital, and found ourselves standing on the same terrace as a photographer had less than a hundred years ago to capture the same angle of the Bethlehem hills. One-way alleys? Tiny streets? "*This is no problem, you just you have to push…*" he offered, in response to my split-second hesitations while driving a big van through the chaotic traffic to our next spot. After a friendly conversation in Arabic with a guy on the street corner, he again led us to the exact location for several photo recreations. We soon had some great shots, and before we knew it, we were back at his house for more coffee. He was fast…and we weren't outrunning the police.

Hebron from the south with Tomb of the Patriarchs in the upper left; Date: 1910–1920

HEBRON

At the core of the biblical narrative of Abraham, Isaac, and Jacob, we find Hebron. It is here that Abraham lived, built an altar to God, and purchased land, including a burial place for his family. Hebron is where Abraham, Sarah, Isaac, Rebekah, Jacob, and Leah are buried. Jewish tradition believes that Adam and Eve are buried here as well.

> *So Abram went to live near the great trees of Mamre at Hebron, where he pitched his tents. There he built an altar to the LORD."*
>
> (Genesis 13:18)

Hebron from the south with Tomb of the Patriarchs in the upper left; Date: 2016

> *While scorning the idea of Jewish colonization, the writer observed that the once populous area between Hebron and Bethlehem was 'now abandoned and desolate' with 'dilapidated towns.'"*

(Alexis, Jonas E., *Christianity and Rabbinic* Judaism, Vol. II, Bloomington, 2013, citing S. Olin, *Travels in Egypt, Arabia Petraea and the Holy Land*, Vol. 2, [New York, 1843], 2 pp. 77–78)

Hebron from the west with the Tomb of the Patriarchs in the center;
Date: 1898–1946

Hebron from the west with the Tomb of the Patriarchs in the center;
Date: 2016

THE MODERN LENS | 77

Jordan Valley from the monastery (above Jericho); Date: 1910–1920

JERICHO

In the Jordan Valley, just north of the Dead Sea, sits the ancient oasis of Jericho. It was near here that Israel first entered the Promised Land and set up camp, observed the Passover, and circumcised those born in the desert before conquering Jericho. Today, the natural springs still flow and provide water for the recent agricultural growth in the area.

> *So Abram went to live near the great trees of Mamre at Hebron, where he pitched his tents."*
>
> (Numbers 22:1)

This image taken from the same vantage point today clearly shows that Jordan Valley has now come to life.

> *(1867) Jericho the accursed lies a moldering ruin today, even as Joshua's miracle left it more than three thousand years ago."*
>
> (Mark Twain, *The Innocents Abroad*, pp. 441–442)

THE MODERN LENS

The Plains of Jericho; Date: 1894

PERSONAL ENCOUNTERS:
Arab Hospitality and Too Much "White Meat"

I have an old picture of Jericho. It is from the late 1800s and shows ruins with a beautiful stone arch surrounded by open plains (above). I actually didn't believe the arch would still be standing after almost 140 years. After approaching a group of locals, one guy took one look at my old photo and said in a thick Arabic accent, *"That's the old sugar mill. Come, I show you."* I rather hesitantly allowed him to get in the front seat of the van. I fully expected that we were probably going for Arabic coffee first at his friend's shop, a concern that proved true. The coffee was amazing as usual, and after some time, I gently prodded him on to "the old sugar mill." When we got there, I was rather stunned. We found the same

The Plains of Jericho; Date: 2016

arch now partially covered with trees and surrounded by buildings and orchards; the empty desolate plains are now full of life.

After taking several photos with the the afternoon sun beating down upon us, our new friend had an idea: heat relief at Elisha's spring! It was cool and refreshing, still flowing from biblical times. After some smiles, friendly hand signals, and broken English conversations with the locals, we were invited to a home for coffee. Not one to turn down Arab hospitality, I happily accepted on behalf of the team.

At the home, we all sat outside around a table under a large fig tree and a warm breeze and learned about life in the "sleepy town" of Jericho. First came the coffee, then the tea, then news that chicken and kebabs were on the way from the butcher. I was asked to help get the grill fired up, and before long, the meats were cooking and the aroma was making my mouth water. Suddenly, our cook began cursing about the kebabs, complaining there was too much "white meat" in the mix. "*White meat…?*" Rather embarrassed and still cursing, he pointed out the "white meat" to me, which I recognized as fat. I assured him that the "white meat" will improve the flavor of the meat and spices, and that it all looked delicious. Dinner didn't even begin until 10:30 p.m., but I am so glad I had ignored my Western sensibilities to excuse our small team "before it got too late" (which is a silly reason in this culture). The kebabs were some of the best I've ever had anywhere…even with the white meat.

Jericho's Jordan Hotel;
Date: 1898-1946

> *Jericho was a 'poor nasty village.'"*
>
> (Henry Maundrell, *The Journal of Henry Maundrell from Aleppo to Jerusalem, 1697*, Bohn's edition [London, 1848]), p. 108)

Jericho's Jordan Hotel;
Date: 2016

THE MODERN LENS | 83

*Shiloh from the South;
Date: 1910–1920*

SHILOH

Before Jerusalem was Israel's spiritual and ruling capital, there was Shiloh. This was where the tribes of Israel gathered to divide the land, celebrate the feasts, the place the Ark of the Covenant sat for over 365 years, and where the Bible said God first revealed His Name. Today, after 4000 years the Jewish community still thrives as they rebuild one of these "forgotten places."

Shiloh from the South;
Date: 2016

> "The whole assembly of the Israelites gathered at Shiloh and set up the tent of meeting there. The country was brought under their control."
>
> (Joshua 18:1)

THE MODERN LENS | 85

Shiloh, Field of the Maidens referring to Judges 19:21;
Date: 1910–1920

Shiloh, Field of the Maidens, the building continues;
Date: 2016

*Shiloh ruins;
Date: 1910–1920*

PERSONAL ENCOUNTERS:
Yisrael Showing Us Israel

Soon after arriving at the Shiloh visitors center and explaining to them our project, we were told to contact a local man who was an experienced tour guide at Shiloh and held many of the old photos of this town. No less than five minutes later, he unexpectedly walked through the door. His scheduled tour had just been cancelled, so he was now suddenly free. His name was Yisrael.

He excitedly gathered his pictures, I grabbed my laptop, and our group of four set out like men (and a

Shiloh ruins; Date: 2016

woman) on a mission. With a satisfied smile, Yisrael led us to spots and angles that would have taken us hours to find on our own, all with a mix of heartfelt pride in the land and the ease of the Jewish shepherds that roamed these hills thousands of years before him. He seemed to project a sense of fulfillment in sharing a location that he loved. He appreciated our sense of purpose and devotion to our mission, and seemed grateful that we weren't just a busload of partially interested tourists. He knew the land and led the way with no hesitation or thought. He would glance at an old picture and say, "Come this way, I show you…" And he was right. Every time.

As we continued our morning, I couldn't help but chuckle at the irony. Yisrael was showing us Israel! Yisrael was showing us ancient Shiloh, the way I imagine God's desire to show Israel to the nations, with love, pride, and the joy of sharing with newcomers. Shiloh is one of the waste cities that has been rebuilt and inhabited. It's growing right now.

Looking down on Shechem (Nablus) and north toward Mount Ebal; Date: 1910–1920

SHECHEM (*Present-day* NABLUS)

Shechem is another biblical site with multiple treasures. Here God spoke to Abram about the land and Abram built an altar. It is the traditional resting place of Joseph when Israel came up out of Egypt. Jacob's well is here, which is where Jesus spoke with the Samaritan "woman at the well" in John 4. After the fall of Jerusalem in AD 70, the Romans renamed Shechem "Flavia Neapolis." Through multiple Muslim conquests since the seventh century, the Arab immigrants had trouble pronouncing the "P" sound, and so it became "Neobolis," and eventually Nablus, as it is still called today.

Looking down on Shechem (Nablus) and north toward Mount Ebal;
Date: 2016

❝ *Abram traveled through the land as far as the site of the great tree of Moreh at Shechem. At that time the Canaanites were in the land. The Lord appeared to Abram and said, 'To your offspring I will give this land.' So he built an altar there to the Lord, who had appeared to him."*

(Genesis 12:6–7)

❝ *Nablus consisted of two streets with many people…"*

(Henry Maundrell, *The Journal of Henry Maundrell from Aleppo to Jerusalem, 1697*, Bohn's edition [London, 1848], pp. 477, 428, 450)

THE MODERN LENS | 91

*Joseph's tomb;
Date 1890–1900*

JOSEPH'S TOMB

> *The entire building [Joseph's tomb] is fast crumbling to ruin, presenting a most melancholy spectacle."*
> (W. M. Thomson, Southern Palestine and Jerusalem [New York: Harper 1880]) 1882: 147)

Joseph's tomb; Date 2016

> " *Few tombs on earth command the veneration of so many races and men of divers creeds as this of Joseph. 'Samaritan and Jew, Moslem and Christian alike, revere it, and honor it with their visits. The tomb of Joseph, the dutiful son, the affectionate, forgiving brother, the virtuous man, the wise Prince and ruler. Egypt felt his influence—the world knows his history.'"*
>
> (Twain, 1869: 412)

THE MODERN LENS

*Joseph's tomb and Mt Gerizim;
Date: 1910–1920*

94 | ISRAEL RISING

Joseph's tomb and Mt Gerizim;
Date: 2016

Herod's Amphitheater; Date: 1890s

SAMARIA (SABASTE)

While Samaria is a region, it was also a city. It is here that King Omri, father of Ahab, built a palace, named the city Samaria, and made it the capital of the northern Kingdom of Israel. Later, during the Roman period, it was given by Augustus to Herod the Great, who rebuilt it and called it Sabaste.

Herod's Amphitheater,
Date: 2016

> ❝ *He bought the hill of Samaria from Shemer for two talents of silver and built a city on the hill, calling it Samaria, after Shemer, the name of the former owner of the hill."*
>
> (1 Kings 16:24)

Samaria, Roman Grand Colonnade; Date 1910–1920

Samaria, Roman Grand Colonnade; Date 2016

Pillars of Roman Basillica; Date: 1898–1946

Pillars of Roman Basillica;
Date: 2016

COASTAL PLAIN

> *The north and south [of the Sharon coastal plain] land is going out of cultivation and whole villages are rapidly disappearing from the face of the earth. Since the year 1838, no less than twenty villages there have been thus erased from the map [by the Bedouin] and the stationary population extirpated.*
>
> (H. B. Tristram, *The Land of Israel: A Journal of Travels in Palestine* [London, 1865] p. 490)

Dizengoff Street looking North; Date: 1934–1939

TEL AVIV

Tel Aviv, Israel's "new city," is a miracle in itself. Today, it's the number one place for tech start-up and research and development outside of silicon valley in California. Amazing tech, medical, security, and agricultural advancements—as well as new developments and discoveries—that are literally changing our modern world are being announced on a regular basis. Just over a hundred years ago, before its founding in 1909 on sand dunes, it didn't exist.

Dizengoff Street looking North; Date: 2016

> *The road leading from Gaza to the north was only a summer track, suitable for transport by camels or carts. No orange groves, orchards or vineyards were to be seen until one reached the Yavneh village. The western part toward the sea was almost a desert. The villages in this area were few and thinly populated."*
>
> (Palestine Royal Commission Report of 1973 [ProQuest Information and Learning Company, 2006] quotes an account of the conditions on the coastal plain along the Mediterranean Sea in 1913.)

Mouth of Yarkon River looking south;
Date: 1940–1946

Mouth of Yarkon River looking south;
Date: 2016

Aerial view of Tel Aviv and Yarkon River; Date: 1920–1946

PERSONAL ENCOUNTERS:
Safety Rules

My small team of three (myself, Elise, and my colleague Michael) arrived at a small airport in the distant sand dunes of Tel Aviv with high expectations. I had never been in a helicopter, let alone one about to fly over Israel for photography, so I couldn't wait to get started. While the chopper was being fueled, we were briefed on helicopter safety by Chaim, the pilot, in a tone that fit a casual coffee shop conversation rather than us all packing into a small flying bubble that would soon be a few thousand feet in the air. "*Ok…ummm…let's see…*" Chaim began in a thick Israeli accent, "*Keep your seat belt on at all times …uhh, keep your hands and feet inside the helicopter at all times.… And…Oh yes, it is best to wait until the rotor blades stop turning before you get out. I think that's it.… Let's go.*" Michael shot a sideways glance at me, which

Aerial view of Tel Aviv and Yarkon River;
Date: 2016

I met with a shrugged smile as we noticed there was no paperwork, no liability release forms to sign. Just three quick "safety" comments that would have fit better at a childhood amusement park ride.

The small four-seater helicopter was made for minimal size and weight, not for comfort. Michael and I squeezed into the small back seats with our knees touching the back of the front seats. We looked at each other and shared a disbelieving chuckle as we reached for the simple seat belts that reminded me of the ones in my old Buick from the 1980s. Elise climbed into the front passenger side, whose door had already been removed for her photography work. We joked about her leaning out the side of the chopper, only supported by her "Buick" seatbelt. But as minimal as the safety features were, Chaim's confident demeanor and ownership of the aircraft assured us we were in the most capable of hands. Soon, we were high above Tel Aviv and ready to recreate the photos of a city's birth and stunning growth in barely a hundred years.

As we flew to new photo destinations, Chaim filled us in on his Israeli Air Force career and how he wanted to find peace with their neighbors, but not at the expense of Israeli security. At that moment, we were over the heartland of Israel and could see the entire width of Israel, from the Jordanian mountains on our left to the Mediterranean Sea on our right. "*As you can see, ours is a small country. . .*" Chaim stated with a smile, "*but it's ours.*" As a man who has defended his nation from the air, I marveled at his sense of personal responsibility. It was if he owned and honored every inch of it.

THE MODERN LENS | 109

Dizengoff Street looking south;
Date: 1934–1939

Reading Power House;
Date: 1934–1939

Dizengoff Street looking south;
Date: 2016

Reading Power House;
Date: 2016

THE MODERN LENS | 111

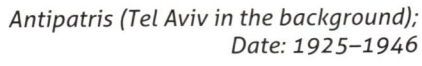
Antipatris (Tel Aviv in the background); Date: 1925–1946

APHEK (ANTIPATRIS)

Aphek was a little-known biblical town in the central coastal plain that hosted more than one battle between Israel and their archnemesis, the Philistines. Later in the first-century BC, Herod the Great built a city there and called it Antipatris, in honor of his father. It was built on the Roman road connecting Jerusalem and Casarea Maritima and hosted Paul while under guard, on his way to Caesarea, mentioned in the New Testament. Today, it's a national park with a view of the Tel Aviv skyline in the background.

Antipatris (Tel Aviv in the background);
Date: 2016

> " Now the Israelites went out to fight against the Philistines. The Israelites camped at Ebenezer, and the Philistines at Aphek." (1 Samuel 4:1)

> " So the soldiers, carrying out their orders, took Paul with them during the night and brought him as far as Antipatris." (Acts 23:31)

THE MODERN LENS | 113

Haifa bay before the harbor completion; Date: 1940–1946

HAIFA

Built on the slopes of the Carmel Mountain range in the northern coastal plain, Haifa has had a settlement history spanning almost 3000 years. While none are noted in the Bible, a variation of the name is found 100 times in the Jewish Talmud. Today, the modern city of Haifa is one of the most populated cities in Israel and has played a large role in Israel's science and technology education and advancements.

*Haifa bay after the harbor completion;
Date: 2016*

> *But where were the inhabitants [Sharon plain]? This fertile plain, which might support an immense population, is almost a solitude.... Day by day we were to learn afresh the lesson now forced upon us, that the denunciations of ancient prophecy have been fulfilled to the very letter— 'the land is left void and desolate and without inhabitants.'"*
>
> (The Reverend Samuel Manning, *Those Holy Fields* [London, 1874] pp. 14–17)

Haifa from Carmel Range;
Date: between 1898–1946

116 | ISRAEL RISING

Haifa from Carmel Range;
Date: 2016

THE MODERN LENS

Haifa panorama;
Date: July 4, 1935

Harbor view and Acco;
Date: 1934–1939

Haifa panorama;
Date: 2016

Harbor view and Acco;
Date: 2016

THE MODERN LENS | 119

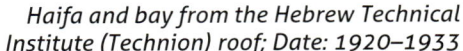

Haifa and bay from the Hebrew Technical Institute (Technion) roof; Date: 1920–1933

PERSONAL ENCOUNTERS:
Help to the Roof

The Technion, or the Israel Institute of Technology, is one of Israel's leading Tech schools. It is based in Haifa and was started in the early part of the twentieth century. Our beautiful old photo from the 1920s was taken from its roof and has the distinctive triangle edging and a great view of the harbor. I had to recreate it, but getting the shot was another story.

What was once a simple climb up two flights of stairs and a ladder to the roof for a photographer a hundred years ago was now a logistical nightmare. The original Technion building is now Israel's National Museum of Science, Technology, and Space and came with a whole new level of bureaucracy and security. After talking up the office chain of command and getting into nicer and nicer offices, we were directed to the workshop out back. That's where we met Ariel.

120 | ISRAEL RISING

Haifa and bay from the Hebrew Technical Institute (Technion) roof; Date: 2016

What was a problem for the office people was no problem for Ariel. He understood the project, the short time frame we had for the photos, and happily accompanied us to the roof. Built like an athlete, Ariel was in his mid-thirties and had made *aliyah* (immigration to Israel) from Virginia in the US just five years ago. We heard about his family back in the States, his pull to this land, and how he made this life-changing step alone. He loved Israel, enjoyed his job, and was a joy to be around. While he insisted his Hebrew was just "okay," it quickly became evident that he did just fine and was well liked by his Hebrew-speaking colleagues. He was optimistically helpful and had a playful smile that never seemed to leave his face—the perfect guy to get us to the roof.

Dressed in all the proper harnesses and hard hats that would have ensured our safety from the apocalypse, we climbed the rather benign ten-foot ladder to the roof just to take a few pictures. We soon had the exact photo angles set up, complete with the same amount of triangle edgings to match the original. We marveled at the change of landscape that lay before us and joked with Ariel about how I had seen far more rooftops in Israel than I ever had in the States. After giving him a couple smooth-tasting Pennsylvania farm country cigars that were grown just a few hours from his childhood home in Virginia as my thanks, we continued on to our next location. I left wishing I had more time to get to know him better and enjoy those cigars together.

Caesarea Harbor from the south, Date: June 1938

CAESAREA

Caesarea was first a small village from the 1 Century BCE, but Herod the Great made vast changes to the city. He built a massive deep water seaport, a Roman city with bathhouses and entertainment venues, and then named it Caesarea in honor of Caesar Augustus. It served as an administrative center of the Judean province under the Roman Empire and played host to several New Testament people and events, including a Roman centurion named Cornelius and Paul's trial and imprisonment. Today, Caesarea is one of the waste places that has been rebuilt and inhabited again, and it is commonly known as the "Beverly Hills of Israel" due to its beautiful beaches, million dollar homes, and several famous residents.

Caesarea Harbor from the south, Date: 2016

> " *At Caesarea there was a man named Cornelius, a centurion in what was known as the Italian Regiment. He and all his family were devout and God-fearing; he gave generously to those in need and prayed to God regularly."*
>
> (Acts 10:1–2)

> " *A ride of half an hour more brought us to the ruins of the ancient city of Caesarea, once a city of two hundred thousand inhabitants, and the Roman capital of Palestine, but now entirely deserted…I laid upon my couch at night, to listen to the moaning of the waves and to think of the desolation around us."*
>
> (B. W. Johnson, *Young Folks in Bible Lands*, 1892 Chapter IV)

THE MODERN LENS

Port, inside southern Crusader walls;
Date: June 1938

Port, inside southern Crusader walls;
Date: June 2016

*Hippodrome, view from the North;
Date: June 1938*

Hippodrome, view from the North;
Date: 2016

THE MODERN LENS

Hippodrome, view from the South;
Date: June 1938

Hippodrome, view from the South;
Date: 2016

Port, inside southern Crusader walls;
Date: June 1938

Port, inside southern Crusader walls;
Date: June 2016

Panorama of Jaffa;
Date: 1894

JAFFA

Jaffa, or "Joppa" in the Bible, has been an ancient port city since the time of the Israelite kings. It was where large supplies of wood from Lebanon were brought to build the Temple, and the Apostle Peter had a vision that led him to Caesarea. Yet the most well-known story identifies Joppa as the port that Jonah went to in order to flee from the Lord's call to send him to Nineveh with a prophetic message. Today its old city has been renovated for tourists and is side by side to the "sister city" of Tel Aviv.

Panorama of Jaffa and Tel Aviv;
Date: 2016

> *But Jonah ran away from the L*ORD *and headed for Tarshish. He went down to Joppa, where he found a ship bound for that port. After paying the fare, he went aboard and sailed for Tarshish to flee from the L*ORD*.."*
>
> Jonah 1:3

> *[Jaffa] has all the appearances of a poor village, and every part of it that we saw was of corresponding meanness."*
>
> (J. S. Buckingham, *Travels in Palestine* [London, 1821], p. 146)

THE MODERN LENS | 133

Jaffa Bazaar;
Date: 1898–1946

Jaffa Bazaar; and Ottoman clock tower
Date: 2016

*Jaffa Port;
Date: 1898–1914*

PERSONAL ENCOUNTERS:
Be Your Own Expert

Today Jaffa is a busy place, unlike life here only 150 years ago. While looking for the angle of an old photo, we found Eli and Sarah. They were eating lunch with a friend at the port and enjoying a much-needed leisurely day at the port, while Grandma was caring for their young son. When we approached Eli and Sarah for directions, they were intrigued by this project and began bubbling over with a surprising amount of local historical info. *"Would you like to help us get out to the breakwater for the next few pics?"* I asked. After a reassuring glance to each other, they enthusiastically agreed, and off we went.

*Jaffa Port;
Date: 2016*

We walked through an open iron gate to a shipyard with a Hebrew sign that read "Do Not Enter." This was also an area that someone had told us just thirty minutes before we couldn't go. As Israel's first Prime Minister, David Ben-Gurion is quoted as saying, "If an expert says it can't be done, get another expert." Such is life in Israel.

We simply walked through the shipyard as if we knew where we were going. We walked around a guy sanding and applying blue paint to the underside of his boat, stepped over some tangled fishing nets, and climbed up the three-foot concrete wall to get on the breakwater. We were soon on our way to recreating some beautiful photos from over a hundred years ago while listening to this fun and helpful couple's story about how they came to Israel. With some things in Israel, just because someone says you can't do something simply means you asked the wrong person or you need to do it yourself.

Older section by the sea;
Date: 1910–1920

Older section by the sea;
Date: 2016

PERSONAL ENCOUNTERS:
Honor in the Desert

In the heart of the Negev desert lie some vineyards that form huge patches of green in a vast landscape of tans and browns. It's a perfect illustration for this book project and a great spot for some photos. As we were capturing some beautiful contrasts in landscape, I met Koren, who was working in the vineyards. Koren was a young guy on vacation from his studies who had the opportunity to earn some shekels. He told me his name means "shining." When I told him that I could tell from his face, he bashfully smiled bigger and said, *"That's what my friends say."* As we were talking, the two-minute siren for Holocaust Remembrance Day sounded from the local town, as it does all over Israel. He took a step back from the vine, bowed his head, and closed his eyes to remember the six million of his family who had died in the Holocaust.

I was struck by the fact that there was no peer pressure for him to do so. We were only a few people in about fifty acres (200 dunam) of vineyards in the middle of an empty desert. He was simply a young man, connected to his land, and connected to his people in a deep way. He didn't have to respond to the siren; he simply reacted to something that was already in him. It is men like this who are simply responding to the deep stirrings within them that are causing the desert to bloom.

THE NEGEV DESERT

Over half of the nation of Israel is desert, but that has not stopped Israel's development, especially in agricultural research and water technologies. After many centuries of destruction and neglect, the Negev desert is coming alive again and quite literally pushing back the desert. Israel is the only country in the world where the desert is shrinking and not expanding. Much of that is a result of the towns seen in this section. As an author and an avid traveler, I find the Negev one of my favorite places in all of Israel.

> **(7th century during Islamic conquests)**
> *Massive soil erosion from the Judaean mountains…western slopes also occurred due to agricultural uprooting during this period…the Negev also experienced the destruction of its agriculture, and the desertion of its villages."*
>
> (Naphtali Lewis, "New Light on the Negev in Ancient Times," *Palestine Exploration Quarterly,* 1948, vol. 80, pp. 116–117)

THE MODERN LENS | 141

*Beersheba, General view;
Date: 1920–1933*

BEERSHEBA

Dating back 4000 years to the time of Abraham, Beersheba was known as the very southern outpost before entering the vast and unforgiving desert. For this reason, the Bible uses the term "from Dan (northern mountains) to Beersheba (the edge of desert in the south)" as a way to describe all of Israel. Today, Beersheba is often called "the capital of the Negev" with its sprawling cityscape, impressive construction boom, and home to one of Israel's largest universities: the Ben-Gurion University of the Negev. Ironically, this was a very difficult location to photograph due to the massive destruction in 1948 during the War of Independence, as the buildings, streets, and photo angles from our pre–1948 photos were simply no longer there.

Beersheba, General view;
Date: 2016

> *Then Abraham returned to his servants, and they set off together for Beersheba. And Abraham stayed in Beersheba."*
>
> (Genesis 22:19)

THE MODERN LENS | 143

Beersheba, main street;
Date: August 1932

Beersheba, main street;
Date: 2016

MITZPE RAMON

Entrance to Mitzpe Ramon,
(courtesy of Mitzpe Ramon Municipality);
Date: 1957

PERSONAL ENCOUNTERS: *Old School Searching*

When Israel became a nation, Mitzpe Ramon simply didn't exist. The town started in the late 1950s and was formed from a camp for the workers who were building the road through the desert to Eilat on the Red Sea. Today, seated on the edge of the huge crater sometimes called the "Israeli Grand Canyon," it's a growing town of 5000, and one of my favorite places in Israel for too many reasons to count. It's so much of a favorite for me, I almost don't want to mention it, because I don't want it to lose its pioneering desert charm.

*Entrance to Mitzpe Ramon,
Date: 2016*

We spent some time digging through the archives "old school style" at the community center and municipality office. No digital files, only dust-covered scrapbooks of old newspaper clippings and yellowed photos.

The older gentleman who helped us with the archives moved here in the late 1960s and watched the town grow from its infancy. He took it on as his personal mission to find the best photos from the town's beginning, clearly enjoying the journey down memory lane. Yet his "journey" was about the speed of a stroll on the weekend after a large meal, and his memory road was remarkably long, but thoroughly enjoyable. We would occasionally hear him let out a chuckle as if he was taken back to the time of the photos, followed by some incoherent mumbling in Hebrew that sounded like a smiling man lost in the good old days. He was a sweet grandfatherly man who offered us coffee, lunch, and his undivided attention.

By evening, we had talked to so many people about old pictures, where they were taken and the interesting stories of the people in them, that half the town knew who we were and what we were doing. We found nothing but warm smiles and inviting people everywhere we went. As these photo comparisons show, this part of the desert is blooming with life in a myriad of ways.

Mitzpe Ramon from the Water tower with the crater in the backround
(courtesy of Mitzpe Ramon Municipality);
Date: 1960s

Mitzpe Ramon, the planting of a JNF Forest
(courtesy of Mitzpe Ramon Municipality):
Date: 1960s

Mitzpe Ramon from the Water tower with the crater in the backround
Date: 2016

Mitzpe Ramon, the JNF Forest
Date: 2016

*Masada, Roman Camps and Dead Sea;
Date: 1910–1920*

MASADA

Masada is a stunning fortress and palace atop an isolated plateau beside the Dead Sea built by Herod the Great. Later, after the destruction of the Temple in AD 7, Jewish zealots and their families overtook the Roman garrison. This led to a long siege of Masada by Roman forces. They built a massive ramp and finally breached the massive fortress walls. Upon entry, the Romans found 960 people dead from a mass suicide, Jewish zealots that chose death over slavery to Rome. Today, it is one of Israel's most popular and amazing attractions.

Masada, Roman Camps and Dead Sea;
Date: 2016

Masada, standing gateway;
Date: 1910–1920

Masada, standing gateway;
Date: 2016

Masada, Storehouses;
Date: 1898–1946

Masada, Storehouses restored;
Date: 2016

THE MODERN LENS | 155

Eilat, outposts
(courtesy of Eilat Museum);
Date: 1950s

EILAT

The region of Eilat is mentioned in the Bible as Ezion-geber and Eloth, which was part of Edom or present-day Jordan. King Solomon built ships in the area, most likely for trade and commerce. Today, Eilat is Israel's southernmost tip and only seaport on the Red Sea. Israel is so narrow at this point that on a clear day from the beach, one can see Egypt to the right and Jordan and Saudi Arabia to the left . Its tropical port atmosphere and major vacation attractions make it a popular destination for Israelis as well as many Europeans.

*Eilat, Israel in the foreground;
Aqaba, Jordan in the background;
Date: 2016*

❝ *King Solomon also built ships at Ezion Geber, which is near Elath in Edom, on the shore of the Red Sea."*

(1 Kings 9:26)

Um Rash Rash; British police station;
(courtesy of Eilat museum);
Date: Nov 21, 1946

PERSONAL ENCOUNTERS:
The Unexpected Museum Manager

While visiting the local museum to ask about photos from Eilat's founding, I was told: *"You need to meet Avi. He started the museum and has everything you need."* Fifteen minutes later, a tall man in his eighties unexpectedly walked into the museum for a meeting. His skin was a deep leathery tan, his white hair made Albert Einstein's mop look stylish, and he had a sharp gaze that peered at us through his big glasses. He wore flip-flops, old shorts, and an open shirt barely buttoned about his navel, exposing various colors of chest hair and a gold chain. He looked more like a beach bum than a museum manager. He gave not a care to the business phrase "dress to impress." This was Avi.

158 | ISRAEL RISING

Um Rash Rash; British police station;
Date: 2016

After being mildly annoyed that the receptionist pointed us out, he turned to us and in a gravelly deep smoker's voice casually asked, "*What may I do for you*?" I introduced myself and quickly explained we were looking for old photos of the area that we planned to recreate for a photo book. After hearing my first two sentences, he interrupted and offered his direct "matter-of-fact" Israeli opinion. "*This is a very amateur book project. People don't care about that. You need to connect it to something historical or even biblical for it to get people's attention.*" When I pushed back and explained that it was historical and biblically based, and that we already had thousands of photos from all over Israel from the late 1800s, he paused and listened. "*Okay, call me this afternoon,*" and off he went.

After a mid-afternoon phone call, we arrived at his house. Avi answered the door wearing less than at our initial meeting, the same old shorts and a cigarette but without the shirt. With the warm hospitality of an old friend, he invited us into his home and his personal study. After serving us some cold drinks, we were soon looking at one of Israel's largest personal photo archives of well over 500,000 photos dating back to the mid-1800s. It was the prized collection of a man who valued every picture as historical documentation of his nation. *"I'll give you whatever you want. Just tell me what you need,"* he offered. After a few hours, we left with a warm handshake, wishes of luck for our book project, and the pictures we needed. It was an honor to spend time with someone who not only had witnessed the changes, but someone who had captured the photos for future generations to see.

Northern shoreline;
Credit Shmulik Taggar;
Date: 1960s

Um Rash Rash protest;
Credit Shmulik Taggar;
Date: 1960s

Northern shoreline;
Date: 2016

Um Rash Rash;
Date: 2016

THE MODERN LENS

Eilat Airport;
(Courtesy of Eilat Museum);
Date: 1960s

Eilat Airport;
Date: 2016

Eilat settlement;
(Courtesy of Eilat Museum);
Date: 1960s

164 | ISRAEL RISING

The town of Eilat;
Date: 2016

Road to Eilat from the west
(courtesy of Eilat Museum);
Date: 1950s

Road to Eilat from the west;
Date: 2016

CENTER

> *Now the district is quite deserted, and you ride among what seem to be so many petrified waterfalls. We saw no animals moving among the stony brakes; scarcely even a dozen little birds in the whole course of the ride.*
>
> (Describing the road between Jaffa and Jerusalem. William Thackeray, *From Jaffa to Jerusalem*, (1844)

Church of the Apparition in Deir el Azhar;
Date: 1941

ABU GHOSH

Through archeology, it was determined that the modern town of Abu Gosh is the location of the biblical town of Kiriath-Jearim, where the Ark of Covenant rested for twenty years, until David sought to bring it to Jerusalem. Today, Abu Ghosh is a model city in Israel, as Jewish and Arab populations have lived peacefully and happily side by side since before 1948.

Church of the Apparition in Deir el Azhar; Date: 2016

> *So the men of Kiriath Jearim came and took up the ark of the Lord. They brought it to Abinadab's house on the hill and consecrated Eleazar his son to guard the ark of the Lord."*
>
> (1 Samuel 7:1)

THE MODERN LENS | 171

View to the Northeast taken from Tel Beth Shemesh; Date: 1931

BETH SHEMESH

Beth Shemesh's history dates back to the Canaanite period, but its most notable biblical event happened during the wheat harvest when two oxen appeared pulling a cart, carrying the stolen Ark of the Covenant. Today, the modern town, which was founded in 1950, is about 30 km (19 miles) west of Jerusalem.

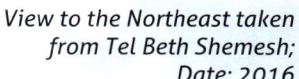

View to the Northeast taken from Tel Beth Shemesh; Date: 2016

> " *Now the people of Beth Shemesh were harvesting their wheat in the valley, and when they looked up and saw the ark, they rejoiced at the sight."*
>
> (1 Samuel 6:13)

Beth Shemesh from the hills of Beit Jamal;
Date: 1920–1933

Beth Shemesh from the hills of Beit Jamal;
Date: 2016

Aerial view looking Southwest;
Date: Nov. 10, 1933

JERUSALEM

Just as the heart is the center of the human body, Jerusalem is the heart in the center of Israel. Perhaps no city on earth has captured the world's attention through the centuries like Jerusalem. Yet, it appears that that was part of the plan.

> *This is what the Sovereign Lord says: This is Jerusalem, which I have set in the center of the nations, with countries all around her."*
>
> (Ezekiel 5:5)

*Aerial view looking Southwest;
Date: 2016*

> In 1835, Alphonse de Lamartine wrote:
> *Outside of the gates of Jerusalem, we saw, indeed, no living object, heard no living sound. We found the same void, the same silence as we should have found before the entombed gates of Pompeii or Herculaneum…complete, eternal silence reigns in the towns, the highways, in the country."*
>
> (Alphonse de Lamartine, *Recollections of the East,* Vol. 1 [London 1845])

Jews 7,120	Jews 28,112	Jews 40,000
Moslems 5,000	Moslems 8,560	Moslems 7,000
Christians 3,390	Christians 8,748	Christians 13,000
Population of Jerusalem, Turkish Census 1844	*Population of Jerusalem, Calendar of Palestine 1895*	*Population of Jerusalem, Travel Guide to Palestine 1906*

THE MODERN LENS | 177

Temple Mount and Western Wall from Southwest;
Date: 1930–1946

Temple Mount and Western Wall from Southwest;
Date: 2016

City of David and Temple Mount from the Southwest;
Date: 1910–1920

Hebron road, southwest of the Old City, looking north;
Date: 1898–1907

City of David and Temple Mount from the Southwest; Date: 2016

Hebron road, southwest of the Old City, looking north; Date: 2016

The "Dung Gate" on the southern end of the old city;
Date: 1940–1946

The "Dung Gate" on the southern end of the old city;
Date: 2016

Hebrew University Campus on Mount Scopus;
Date: 1925–1946

Hebrew University Campus on Mount Scopus;
Date: 2016

THE MODERN LENS

On top of the Jaffa Gate, Road from Jerusalem to Bethlehem looking South; Date: 1894

Exterior of Tower of David; Date: 1894

On top of the Jaffa Gate, Road from Jerusalem to Bethlehem looking South; Date: 2016

Exterior of Tower of David; Date: 2016

Mount of Offense, (present-day village of Silwan) Southside of the old city;
Date: 1894

Mount of Offense, (present-day village of Silwan) Southside of the old city;
Date: 2016

YMCA, King David hotel, Aerial from Southwest;
Date 1933–1946

*YMCA, King David hotel, Aerial from Southwest;
Date 2016*

Central Valley at the Dung Gate; Date: 1910–1920

PERSONAL ENCOUNTERS: *Don't Give Up*

Some pictures came easy, others not so much. We wanted to capture this angle (above) taken from on top of the Dung Gate that is inside the archeology park, looking back towards the Kotel (Western Wall Plaza). I spoke to the guy at the park entrance, showed him the photo we wanted to recreate, and told him it would only take me five minutes after jumping a fence and climbing on top of the gate. However, due to the vantage point, there were several security cameras in this restricted area. Seemingly happy to push us off, they sent us to the police station in the Western Wall Plaza. After hearing my "kindest" explanation, the police said they just own the cameras, and told us we had to go talk to the Western Wall Rabbi's office.

Entrance to the Western Wall; Date: 2016

After hearing my "trying to be kind" explanation, the Rabbi's office said it wasn't in the actual plaza. It wasn't their responsibility, so they told us to go back to the archeological park. Soon I found myself back at the same desk talking to the same guy as from the beginning. Seeing my persistence, he softened a little and pointed me in the direction of his manager's office.

Upon finding the office and giving the manager my "mildly irritated from the runaround" explanation of why I needed access to that specific spot, she replied, *"We do allow that in certain situations for 400 shekels ($100) an hour." "Look."* I said, half exasperated and half pleading, *"I'm not paying 400 shekels. I just need five minutes and your permission to hop the fence and to know that the police won't come running when I do."* Much to my surprise, she sat back in her chair, shrugged, and said, "Okay." Mildly shocked, I confirmed, *"It's okay?"* She nodded with a partial smile, and I quickly left before anyone could change their minds.

As we hurried back to the Dung Gate, a security guard who had watched this whole process spoke up to give his unsolicited opinion. *"This is going to be a good book,"* he said. Taken aback, I asked him why. *"Lots of people can take pictures, but you know where you need to go and don't stop until you get there. This is going to be a good book."*

THE MODERN LENS | 193

Jerusalem train station;
Date: 1898–1914

*Looking Northwest
from Mount of Olives;
Date: 1910–1920*

Jerusalem train station, renovated to shops and cafes; Date: 2016

Looking Northwest from Mount of Olives; Date: 2016

Dome of the Rock and Western Wall;
Date: 1898–1946
[probably after 1927]

Jewish Wailing Place
(Western Wall);
Date: approx. 1894

Dome of the Rock and Western Wall;
Date: 2016

Jewish Wailing Place (Western Wall);
Date: 2016

Mosque of Omar (Dome of the Rock);
Date: 1894

Mosque of Omar (Dome of the Rock);
Date: 2016

THE MODERN LENS | 199

CONCLUSION

We have read the prophecy's details. We have scanned history and have noticed a trend of what happens to the land with and without Jewish sovereignty. We have viewed the old photos that give credence to the eyewitness accounts throughout the centuries. Through visual comparisons, we have seen how dramatically the land has changed since Israel became a nation, just as the prophecy foretold. No other people group or national homeland in history can compare to this experience.

These unique circumstances that coincide with Ezekiel 36 lead us to one of two conclusions: (1) This is a wild and compelling coincidence that is an anomaly in human history; or (2) Something supernatural or divine is at work behind the scenes. While this conclusion may be solely the decision of the reader, all these events are clearly linked to the prophecy.

If we look back at the Ezekiel 36 passage, it appears that God said He would take personal responsibility in this process and explained exactly what He would do:

- He will turn towards you (the land and the people). (v. 9)
- He will multiply man and beast on the land. (v. 11)
- He will cause Israel to walk the land and take possession of the land. (v. 12)
- He will not let the insults towards the land continue. (v. 15)
- He will sanctify His name among the nations as a result of this process. (v. 23)
- He will gather Israel from the nations and bring them back to their own land. (v. 24)
- He will give Israel a new heart, a new spirit and bring a cleansing. (vv. 26–27)
- He will not bring a famine on the land. (v. 29)
- He will multiply the fruit of the trees and the increase of the fields. (v. 30)
- He will enable Israel to rebuild and dwell in the cities. (v. 33)
- He encourages Israel to ask Him to do all of this. (v. 37)

For many of these points, we have seen the beginnings of tangible fulfillment in this book. Some points are more difficult to quantify. Yet regardless of where we are at in this process of restoration, one thing is clear—something miraculous is happening, when viewed through the eyes of history. Ezekiel 36 tells us that when these changes start happening, God is the One doing it.

By the end of this prophecy, God clearly explains why He is reviving the land:

They will say, "This land that was laid waste has become like the garden of Eden; the cities that were lying in ruins, desolate and destroyed, are now fortified and inhabited." Then the nations around you that remain will know that I the LORD have rebuilt what was destroyed and have replanted what was desolate. I the LORD have spoken, and I will do it." (Ezekiel 36:35–36)

If God's original everlasting covenant with Abraham, regarding "His chosen people," is still valid, the land will give testimony to that as well. No other group of people in human history has been planted on a piece of land, forcibly removed; then returned after seventy years to the same piece of land; then forcibly removed again and scattered to the ends of the earth for 2000 years; then return a second time to the exact same piece of real estate as an identifiable people with the same customs, language, and beliefs as their ancient ancestors. And all the while, their homeland ceased to produce *until* their return. If God's covenant promise to Abraham and Ezekiel's prophecy are to be believed in a literal way, then through the land's miraculous transformation, we are beginning to witness one of the greatest demonstrations of God's faithfulness to His promises in the last several thousand years. The prophecy states that at some point the land's transformation will be so stunning in the scope of its history that the nations will recognize that only God could have done it. According to the Scriptures, He is calling the nations to Himself, and He's using the land of Israel to do it. I believe it's happening right now.

It is not simply the land whose revival was foretold, but the people as well. Three times in Ezekiel 36, the idea of a national "cleansing" is connected to the return of the Jewish people to their land and the physical renewal of the land itself. In fact, many times throughout other prophetic scriptures, when the return of the Jewish people to the land is mentioned, so is the arrival of the Messiah, who will bring about a restoration to God. The unveiling of the Messiah in Jerusalem is faithfully expected by both Jews and Christians. At the end of this passage, there is a connection between a cleansing and the land becoming like the Garden of Eden again. The Garden was not simply a beautiful place, but a special place where God dwelled with man, in his sinless state. Verses 24 and 25 state that He will gather the people back from the nations to their own land, and THEN the cleansing comes. If the people are returning now, and the land is physically responding as well, then the Messiah and the cleansing are not far behind.

Regardless of our personal beliefs, history has shown us that what is happening in Israel has never been seen before. I expect in another fifty years we'll be able to look back at these comparison photos and marvel at how much more the land has blossomed, been recreated, and built up within that time frame. God is faithful to His people, this land, and to all the people and nations that will recognize His hand in these amazing transformations. While I am sure we have not seen its fullness yet, we are watching Ezekiel's prophecy coming to pass.

> **"This land that was a wasteland has become like the garden of Eden. The waste, desolate and ruined cities are fortified and inhabited."**
>
> (Ezekiel 36:35)

REFERENCE
Historical eyewitness accounts of the land from 4th–19th century

4th Century (Byzantine Empire)

As Christianity spread and became the state religion of the Byzantine Empire, the first of the Christian pilgrims began venturing to the "holy land" to see Jerusalem and other sites of Christian significance. The most famous of these were Helena, Paula and Eustochium. Many of their letters record what they found and experienced. In her writings, Paula contrasts the wealth of Rome to the poverty she found in Bethlehem:

> *"Where are spacious porticoes? Where are gilded ceilings? Where are houses decorated by the sufferings and labours of condemned wretches? Where are halls built by the wealth of private men on the scale of palaces…. In the village of Christ … all is rusticity, and except for psalms, silence…. Indeed, we do not think of what we are doing or how we look, but see only that for which we are longing."* (Stewart, A; 1896)

6th Century (Byzantine Empire)

While having its beginnings in the fifth century, Jewish persecution and destruction of property were openly encouraged in the sixth century.

> *"Jews couldn't own slaves (making agriculture difficult). They couldn't build new synagogues.... Jews were forbidden to read the torah or any other book in Hebrew … Justinian encouraged Christians to destroy synagogues, stores, and Jewish houses."* (www.Jewishvirtuallibrary.org/jsource/history/byzantine1.html)

7th Century (Persian Empire/Islamic rule)

After a short Persian conquest of the land, the Islamic invasions began.

> *"The whole Gaza region up to Cesarea was sacked and devastated in the campaign of 634. Four thousand Jewish, Christian, and Samaritan peasants, who were defending their land were massacred. The villages of the Negev were pillaged…. Sophronius* [the patriarch of Jerusalem], *in his sermon on the Day of the Epiphany 636, bewailed the destruction of the churches and monasteries, the sacked towns, the fields laid waste, the villages burned down by the nomads who were overthrowing the country."* (Bat Ye'or, *The Decline of Eastern Christianity Under Islam* (Farleigh Dickinson University Press, 1996))

Historian Carl Voss explains the effects of Arab conquests in the region that began in the seventh century and continued for the following 1200 years:

> "In the twelve and a half centuries between the Arab conquest in the seventh century and the beginnings of the Jewish return in the 1880s, Palestine was laid waste. Its ancient canal and irrigation systems were destroyed and the wondrous fertility of which the Bible spoke vanished into desert and desolation... Under the Ottoman empire of the Turks, the policy of disfoliation continued; the hillsides were denuded of trees and the valleys robbed of their topsoil." (Voss, *The Palestine Problem Today, Israel and Its Neighbors* (Beacon Press, 1953), p. 13)

8th Century (Various Arab rule)

Under Islamic rule, Jews and Christians were forced to pay a special infidel (*Dhimmi*—a non-Muslim person or literally "protected person") tax referred to as the *jizya*. Jewish historian Bat Ye'or explains the financial oppression that took place throughout eighth century Palestine, which devastated the *dhimmi* Jewish and Christian population:

> "Overtaxed and tortured by the tax collectors, the villagers fled into hiding or emigrated into towns." (Bat Ye'or, *The Decline of Eastern Christianity Under Islam*)

This flight from heavy taxes led many to leave their homes and fields as detailed by an eight-century monk in 774:

> "The men scattered, they became wanderers everywhere; the fields were laid waste, the countryside pillaged; the people went from one land to another." (Chronique de Denys de Tell—Mahre, translated from the Syriac by Jean—Baptiste Chabot [Paris, 1895], English translation in: Bat Ye'or, *The Decline of Eastern Christianity Under Islam*)

9th Century (Various Arab rule)

> "The Greek chronicler Theophanes provides a contemporary description of the chaotic events which transpired after the death of the caliph Harun al-Rashid in 809 C.E. He describes Palestine as the scene of violence, rape, and murder, from which Christian monks fled to Cyprus and Constantinople." (Moshe Gil, *A History of Palestine*, 634–1099)

> "The Muslim historian Baladhuri (d. 892 C.E.), maintained that 30,000 Samaritans and 20,000 Jews lived in Caesarea alone just prior to the Arab Muslim conquest; afterward, all evidence of them disappears. Archaeological data confirms the lasting devastation wrought by these initial jihad conquests, particularly the widespread destruction of synagogues and churches from the Byzantine era, whose remnants are still being unearthed. The total number of towns was reduced from fifty-eight to seventeen in the red sand hills and swamps of the western coastal plain (i.e., the Sharon)." (Al-Baladhuri, *The Origins of the Islamic State* [Kitah Futuh al-Buldan], translated by Philip K. Hitti [London, Longman, Greens, and Company, 1916], p. 217, Constantelos, "Greek Christian and Other Accounts of the Moslem Conquests of the Near East," pp. 127–28.

10th Century (Various Arab rule)

In 985, over 300 years into Muslim rule in the region, the Arab writer Muqaddasi lamented about the Muslim population in Jerusalem:

> *"The mosque is empty of worshipers ... The Jews constitute the majority of Jerusalem's population."* (Muqaddasi, quoted by Erich Kahler who cites this statement from *Knowlege of Crimes*, p.167, in *The Jews Among the Nations* [New York: F. Ungar, 1967], p. 144)

11th Century (Various Arab Rule/ Crusader conquest)

> *"Muslim Turcoman rule of Palestine for the nearly three decades just prior to the Crusades (1071–1099 C.E.) was characterized by such unrelenting warfare and devastation, that an imminent. End of Days atmosphere was engendered."* (Moshe Gil, *A History of Palestine*, 634–1099), pp. 412–416)

> *"A contemporary poem by Solomon ha-Kohen b. Joseph, believed to be a descendant of an illustrious family of Palestinian Jews of priestly descent, writes of his recollection of the previous Turcoman conquest of Jerusalem during the eighth decade of the 11th century. He speaks of destruction and ruin, the burning of harvests, the razing of plantations, the desecration of cemeteries, and acts of violence, slaughter, and plunder."* (Julius Greenstone, in his essay, "The Turcoman Defeat at Cairo," The *American Journal of Semitic Languages and Literatures*, Vol. 22, 1906, pp. 144–175, provides a translation of this poem[excerpted, pp. 164–165] by Solomon ha-Kohen b. Joseph.)

As the Crusader era entered the Holy Land, not much had changed. William of Tyre, a twelfth-century clergyman, described the crusaders' entry into Jerusalem in the year 1099:

> *"They went together through the streets with their swords and spears in hand. All them that they met they slew and smote right down, men, women, and children, sparing none.... They slew so many in the streets that there were heaps of dead bodies, and one might not go nor pass but upon them that so lay dead.... There was so much bloodshed that the channels and gutters ran all with blood, and all the streets of the town were covered with dead men."* (William of Tyre, from *A History of Deeds Done Beyond the Sea* [Columbia University Press, 1943])

12th Century (Crusader kingdom of Jerusalem)

Almost 100 years later in 1191, the Crusader battles and bloodshed were ongoing. During the conquest of Acre, one author describes the brutal fate of 2,700 Arabs in that city:

> *"Richard's men began to carry out his orders to kill them all. This time the children were not saved for the slave market, but were butchered with their fathers and mothers...The killing completed, Richard's army started back to the city, while on the top of the hill a few loot-crazed butchers lurched from one body to another with their bloody knives, hastily disemboweling corpses to recover any gold pieces that might have been swallowed for concealment..."* (Robinson, *Dungeon, Fire and Sword*, M Evans & Co, 1991)

13th Century (Crusader defeat/ Mamluks conquest)

14th Century (Mamluks Rule)

After the expulsion of the Crusaders and following Mamluks' rule, the land continued to be decimated, and the overwhelming poverty continued:

> "Having ejected the Crusaders, the Mamluks wanted to prevent their return. They therefore destroyed the Crusader beachheads—Palestine's coastal cities. But destruction of the port cities deprived the inland cities of commercial access to the sea and to other international trade routes, causing a depression...Economic conditions were poor; Palestine shared with other lands in droughts, famines, earthquakes, epidemics, high taxes, high prices, government corruption, and attacks by Bedouins and bandits." (http://www.al-bushra.org/America/ap1.html)

15th Century (Mamluk Rule)

> "The Mamluk tenure throughout Israel (Palestine) and Jerusalem became increasingly oppressive towards Jews and especially Christians as their tenure unfolded. Those who refused to convert to Islam were subject to severe legal and social discrimination and even had to pay special taxes. The Mamluks allowed their communities to morph into lawlessness against Jews and Christians in the form of protests, riots, and anarchy. The Mamluk control over Israel (Palestine) and Jerusalem was ended by the Ottomans in 1517." (Christians-standing-with-Israel.org/mamluks-map-jerusalem.html)

16th Century (Mamluk Rule/Ottoman Empire)

Despite the conflicts and poverty, pilgrims still came and journaled what they saw and experienced:

> [Jerusalem in 1590] "Nothing there is to bescene but a little of the old walls, which is yet Remayning and all the rest is grasse, mosse and Weedes much like to a piece of Rank or moist Grounde." (Gunner Edward Webbe, *Palestine Exploration Fund, Quarterly Statement*, p. 86, cited in de Haas, *History* p. 338)

> "'A house of robbers, murderers, the inhabitants are Saracens [Nazareth].... It is a lamentable thing to see thus such a town. We saw nothing more stony, full of thorns and desert'" (De Haas, *History*, p. 337, citing *Palestine Exploration Fund, Quarterly Statement*, 1925)

17th Century (Ottoman Empire)

Again, after a change in sovereignty in the land, historian Bernard Lewis reports that not much had changed regarding poverty and the treatment of the land:

> "Harsh, exorbitant, and improvident taxation led to a decline in cultivation, which was sometimes permanent. The peasants, neglected and impoverished, were forced into the hands of money-lenders and speculators, and often driven off the land entirely. With the steady decline in bureaucratic efficiency during the seventeenth and eighteenth centuries...the central government ceased to exercise any check or control over agriculture and village affairs, which were left to the unchecked rapacity of the tax-farmers,

the leaseholders, and the bailiffs of court nominees." (Bernard Lewis, *The Emergence of Modem Turkey* [London, 1961], p. 33)

18th Century (Ottoman Empire)

Starting in the eighteenth and nineteenth centuries, multiple travelers to the region began noticing a dramatic decline in population:

Thomas Shaw wrote that the land in Palestine was *"lacking in people to till its fertile soil."* (Thomas Shaw, *Travels and Observations Relating to Several Parts of Barbary and the Levant* [London, 1767], p. 331ff)

". . . upwards of three thousand two hundred villages were reckoned; but, at present, the collector can scarcely find four hundred. Such of our merchants as have resided there twenty years have themselves seen the greater part of the environs . . . become depopulated. The traveler meets with nothing but houses in ruins, cisterns rendered useless, and fields abandoned. Those who cultivated them have fled . . ." (Count Constantine F. Volney, *Travels Through Syria and Egypt in the Years 1783, 1784, 1785,* London, 1788 Vol. 2, p. 147)

"By the end of the 18th century, much of the land was owned by absentee landlords and leased to impoverished tenant farmers. The land was poorly cultivated and a widely neglected expanse of eroded hills, sandy deserts, and malarial marshes encroached on what was left of agricultural land. Taxation was crippling, with even its few trees being taxed. (Clarence Wagner, *365 Fascinating Facts About Israel,* #311C- 2006)

As we'll see in the early photos and records in the eighteenth century, the population in the region was not growing, but declining under Ottoman taxation. In 1857, the British Consul in Palestine reported:

"The country is in a considerable degree empty of inhabitants and therefore its greatest need is that of a body of population . . . " (James Finn to the Earl of Clarendon, Jerusalem, September 15, 1857, F.O. 78/1294 (Pol. No. 36)

"In the 1860s, it was reported that 'depopulation is even now advancing.'" (J. B. Forsyth, *A Few Months in the East,* Quebec, 1861), p. 188)

"Jerusalem consisted of 'a large number of houses . . . in a dilapidated and ruinous state,' and 'the masses really seem to be without any regular employment.' The 'masses' of Jerusalem were estimated at less than 15,000 inhabitants, of whom more than half the population were Jews." (No. 238, "Report of the Commerce of Jerusalem During the Year 1863," F.O. 195/808, May 1864)

In 1866, W. M. Thomson writes: *"How melancholy is this utter desolation. Not a house, not a trace of inhabitants, not even shepherds, to relieve the dull monotony . . . Much of the country through which we have been rambling for a week appears never to have been inhabited, or even cultivated; and there are other parts, you say, still more barren."* (W. M. Thomson, *The Land and the Book,* London: T. Nelsons & Sons, 1866; and Thompson, *Southern Palestine and Jerusalem* [New York: Harper 1880])

Colonel C. R. Conder, who made frequent visits to Palestine, commented in the book *Heth and Moab* on the continuing population decline within the nine- or ten-year interim between his visits:

> *"The Peasantry who are the backbone of the population, have diminished most sadly in numbers and wealth."* (Colonel C.R. Conder, *Heth and Moab*, London, 1883 pp. 380, 376.

David Landes summarized the causes of the rapid decline of the number of inhabitants: *"As a result of centuries of Turkish neglect and misrule, following on the earlier ravages of successive conquerors, the land had been given over to sand, marsh, the anopheles mosquito, clan feuds, and Bedouin marauders. A population of several millions had shrunk to less than one tenth that number—perhaps a quarter of a million around 1800, and 300,000 at mid-century."* (David Landes, "P," *Commentary*, February, 1976, pp. 48–49)

In 1881, the British cartographer Arthur Penrhyn Stanley surveyed the bleak landscape and wrote:

> *"In Judea it is hardly an exaggeration to say that for miles and miles there was no appearance of life or habitation."* (Arthur Penrhyn Stanley, *Sinai and Palestine*, London: John Murray, 1881, p. 118)

> *"No national union and no national spirit has prevailed there. The motley impoverished tribes which have occupied it have held it as mere tenants at will, temporary landowners, evidently waiting for those entitled to the permanent possession of the soil."* (Sir John William Dawson, 1888, *Modern Science in Bible Lands* [New York, 1890], pp. 449–450)

> *"I traveled through sad Galilee in the spring, and I found it silent.... . As elsewhere, as everywhere in Palestine, city and palaces have returned to the dust. This melancholy of abandonment weighs on all the Holy Land."* (French writer, Pierre Loti, *La Galilee*, Paris, 1895), pp. 37–41)